· POPULAR ·
· COLLECTABLES ·

glass

Muriel M. Miller

GUINNESS PUBLISHING

Dedication . . .
To Dave Barker with love,
gratitude – and a promise

Editor: Honor Head
Picture Research: Julie O'Leary
Design and Layout: Steve Leaning
Photographer: Peter Greenhalf

Published in Great Britain by Guinness
Publishing Ltd, 33 London Road,
Enfield, Middlesex

Typeset in Caslon Old Style by
Ace Filmsetting Ltd, Frome, Somerset
Printed and bound in Italy by New
Interlitho SpA, Milan

**British Library Cataloguing in
Publication Data**
Miller, Muriel M.
    popular collectables, glass.
    1. Glassware
    I. Title
    748.2

ISBN 0-85112-903-X

contents

—— FEATURES ——

introduction

Many antiques books on glass are expensive encyclopedias which contain much that is unnecessary for the new or modest collector. This book is intended to help with information that is presented in an informed but easy-to-digest manner. The A to Z listing is ideal for quick reference, and the glossary explains terms peculiar to glass which might be strange to the beginner. Historical details are given with each entry, and approximate price bands, where appropriate, are intended to guide the collector who is on a limited budget.

Glass is a notoriously difficult field for the beginner. Dating and identifying items can be a problem as glass, other than press-moulded glass, was rarely marked with the maker's trademark. The book gives useful pointers for recognition, aided by numerous colour illustrations.

As early glass can be prohibitively priced, the book concentrates mainly on glass from the mid-19th century and later. However, expensive glass such as that made by leading glassmakers such as Tiffany, Lalique, and Gallé is not ignored, as their ideas and designs influenced other glassmakers. Tiffany's Favrile glass, for example, led to the mass-production of Carnival glass in both America and England, while Lalique's opalescent glass was copied by James A. Jobling in great quantities.

There is a wealth of useful advice in the book on what to look out for when buying, and how to choose your piece: for instance, glass should always be examined with the eyes closed, as any damage is more easily detected by sensitive fingertips. Stoppers in decanters were always ground to fit exactly and any looseness can indicate a 'marriage'. Is it worth buying damaged glass? How can one clean dirty bottles? How do you dry a decanter after washing? All these questions are answered, plus many more.

Late 19th century press-moulded comport, 9in diameter. Made in two parts and welded together; £30–£60.

Pressed glass often bears the maker's trademark, or a registered design number, and these can help with the dating or identification of glass. A comprehensive listing of both these is included in the book. A brief history of some of the major manufacturers is also incorporated, with information on how to recognise their work.

Bargains can be found at boot fairs and flea markets if the buyer has the skill and knowledge to recognise them. Buying from regular and/or specialist dealers at antiques fairs is safer when buying more expensive or collector's items. These dealers are only too willing to guide and advise the beginner.

Auctions are well worth attending, especially small local sales. Prices are generally lower than at antiques fairs as dealers are not prepared to pay too high a price for an item on which they have to make a profit when selling.

If a lot is marked A/F in the catalogue, this means 'as found' or 'at fault' and indicates that the piece is damaged in some way. However, damage is not always listed and it is important to check glass carefully while viewing, as once the hammer has fallen, there is no redress. The rule of 'caveat emptor' or 'let the buyer beware' holds fast. It is also important to set a price limit and stick to it. It is only too easy to be carried away in the excitement of bidding.

Some Victorian glass is now being reproduced and the book advises where this might occur, what to look for, and how to avoid making an expensive mistake. Above all, this book has been written to help make your collecting more interesting, rewarding and enjoyable.

Set of decanter and two liqueur glasses by Gallé in amber glass with enamel and gilt decoration in the design of a butterfly, plants and insects c.1880. Height 2¾in and 7½in; £1000+.

a

Small press-moulded glass plate; £20–£50.

· AMERICAN ·
· LACY · GLASS ·

This American pressed glass (see PRESS-MOULDED GLASS) was made extensively at the Boston and Sandwich Glass Company in Massachusetts from about 1830. The name Sandwich Glass has now become generic, although this type of patterned glass was also made at the New England Glass Company, the Brooklyn Flint Glass Works and other glasshouses.

The pattern that was pressed into the glass was set against a background of stippling which had originally been intended to cover the shear marks where the glass was removed from the machine. However, it proved to give such an attractive lacy effect, transforming the rather basic patterns, that it became standard.

Wares were usually made in clear glass, although coloured examples in blue, amethyst, amber, clear yellow, opaque white and opalescent can sometimes be found. Patterns laid on the stippled background included leaf and flower motifs, shells, hearts, chains and scrolls, stars, triangles and other geometric designs. Some commemorative (q.v.) items were produced, such as portrait plates, souvenir plates, and those made to mark a significant event, maybe the launching of a new shipping line, for example.

Most popular with collectors are cup plates. These small flat plates were intended to protect the table top or cloth from hot coffee or tea cups. The dished saucer that also accompanied the cup was used to cool the tea or coffee prior to drinking it.

Cup plates are not too difficult to find and will cost about £15–£20 upwards, depending on the pattern.

When buying lacy glass the beginner should be careful not to confuse it with British Victorian pressed glass, some of which also had a stippled background but was generally less ornate than its American counterpart. Only by handling both can the necessary knowledge be gained.

· ART · DECO · · GLASS ·

Art Deco is derived from the name of the exhibition held in France in 1925 – The Paris Exposition des Arts Decoratifs – and the style continued through the 1930s until about 1939. The post-war years saw a rebellion against all the strictures of World War I. A gaiety, almost a frenzy, and a craving for anything new and extraordinary was the order of the day. Designs contrasted strongly with those of Art Nouveau (q.v.). Gone were the flowing and sinuous decorative lines; shapes now became angular and geometric. Colours were brash and bold, orange combined with red, for example, on ceramics; red and black on glass.

The French designer, René Lalique

Unusual French goblet with etched and enamelled designs of naked women and peacocks c.1920–30. Height 7¾in; £400–£500.

Paperweight in the shape of a perch in clear glass with an etched finish c.1930. Signed Lalique. Height 4in; £750–£1000.

a

(q.v.) created glass objects that followed the new trend. His glass car mascots are among the finest ever seen, and his 'Spirit of the Wind' shows a girl's head in profile, her hair streaming out behind in a geometric 'fan' shape. Glass figures produced by various other factories were aggressive in pose, abandoned in their semi-nudity.

In Britain, manufacturers experimented with new techniques. Monart (q.v.) produced glass that was swirled and spiralled with colours of pink, red, green and yellow. Similar work was carried out by the Gray-Stan factory (q.v.) and they also used a Nailsea type (q.v.) of decoration where white and coloured glass was pulled up into a herringbone pattern. Keith Murray, a noted designer, was under contract to Stevens & Williams (q.v.) and they produced a range of glass that was sold under the Murray name. Jobling (q.v.) made pressed glass items in imitation of Lalique's opalescent glass and this was moulded with fruit, flowers, fish or birds.

Perfume bottles (see COMMERCIAL PERFUME BOTTLES; SCENT BOTTLES) were made to complement the new 'Jazz Age'. The geometrically-shaped bottles were sometimes accompanied by huge stoppers of triangular or plume design. Others would have sunburst or zig-zag patterns moulded into the glass body. When buying these, it is advisable to go to a reputable dealer, as they are being very accurately reproduced today.

The drinking of cocktails became popular, and glasses and shakers were made in clear glass of formal shape, decorated with slashes of vivid colour (see COCKTAIL GLASSES AND SHAKERS). The glasses were invariably stemmed with shallow, flared bowls.

Bowl-shaped flower holders were

French vase in brown glass with raised pattern of overlapping circles c.1930. Height 7in; £250+.

made in opaque pink, green and blue and the central holder was often composed of a female figure. This gave the illusion of a maiden rising from a sea of flowers when the container was filled. These are still moderately priced and can be found for £15–£30. Check the colour match between the central container and the bowl when buying in order to avoid a 'marriage'.

Tazzas (q.v.) were made in opaque glass, the dish or plate being supported by a chromed nude girl in a dancing pose. Many items were made in Cloud glass (q.v.) and were attractively streaked in various colours.

Trinket sets also followed the new fashion, with a clear, dark amber being a popular colour, as well as pink, blue and green. These too can be found cheaply at about £20–£40, although the design will affect the price – those of a more Art Deco shape commanding higher prices.

· ART · GLASS ·

It is generally recognised that the making of art glass began in the mid-19th century, and it aroused a great deal of interest when it was exhibited in Britain at the Great Exhibition of 1851. Up until 1845, the tax on glass had successfully smothered any attempts at experimentation in form and design, but now artists and designers were able to

French Art Deco vase with a frieze of classical figures, by Georges de Feure c.1920. Height 7in; £250+.

Deep amber bowl with an iridescent finish c.1900. Diameter 15in; £100–£150.

Pair of small vases c. 1900 with silvered inclusions and an iridescent surface. £70–£100 the pair.

give free rein to their ideas. This culminated in the forming of several Guilds and Societies, all of which played their part in influencing the design of glass.

Sir Henry Cole was perhaps the first exponent of the Arts and Crafts movement, and he established Summerby's Art Manufactures in 1847. The Century Guild was established in 1882 by Arthur Heygate Mackmurdo, a disciple of William Morris and John Ruskin. Another disciple of the latter two men was Charles Robert Ashbee, and he founded the Guild and School of Handicraft in 1887. In 1896, the Arts and Crafts Exhibition Society was formed with Walter Crane, a friend of William Morris, as its first president.

While these various guilds were not chiefly concerned with glassmaking, they had an important influence on the designers in that industry. Thomas Webb (q.v.) produced, under licence, a new glass with subtle shadings of pink and yellow which he called Burmese Glass (q.v.). This had first been made in America by the Mount Washington

Glass Company. Webb also experimented with cameo glass (q.v.) and became a leading exponent in England. John Northwood (q.v.) produced a copy of the Portland Vase in cameo glass.

Again in America, Tiffany (q.v.) was manufacturing Favrile, a type of iridescent glass. Tiffany, like Emile Gallé (q.v.), was to become renowned for his Art Nouveau designs.

In France, the new movement was even more vigorous and François Eugene Rousseau used enamelling to great effect. He also produced exquisite cameo vases based on early Chinese snuff bottles. His work influenced men such as Gallé whose cameo glass work was later to figure so prominently in the Art Nouveau period (see ART NOUVEAU GLASS).

A process rather similar in appearance to carved, cased glass was that of 'pâte-de-verre' (meaning literally a glass paste). Powdered glass was mixed with an adhesive and then formed in a mould in cameo or relief form. The technique is also known as 'pâte-de-riz' and 'pâte-de-cristal'.

Many French glassmakers used the lost wax process for their work. The wax model was encased by a mould and then heated. The wax ran out of the mould leaving behind an exact replica shape. This new mould was then filled with molten glass.

Some artists and designers turned to the past for their inspiration, and Persian, Arabic, Roman and even early Japanese designs were copied or adapted. Philipe-Joseph Brocard of Paris became fascinated by Islamic glass and copied the ancient techniques and formulas. He produced some excellent pieces which were exhibited at the World Exhibition in Paris in 1867.

French glass vase by Brocard with painted enamelled decoration in Islamic style, having a freize of script in blue and red enamels c.1875/80. Height 5in; £1000+.

· ART · · NOUVEAU · · GLASS ·

Cranberry vase with iridescent finish and gilt collar. Height 4in; £50–£70.

The name Art Nouveau or new art is thought to have been taken from the gallery in Paris owned by Samuel Bing, and called 'La Maison de l'Art Nouveau'. However, in France the style became known as 'le style moderne', while the Germans called it 'youth style' or Jugendstil. The period for Art Nouveau falls roughly between about 1880 and 1914, and it evolved from (and overlapped) the Arts and Crafts movement (see ART GLASS), but with designs becoming more rhythmic and flowing. Straight lines were never used – the artists concentrated on swirling, linear curves.

There was great interest in the naturalistic and plant forms, and many of the leading Art Nouveau artists and designers, such as Emile Gallé (q.v.), Christopher Dresser, and Charles Rennie Mackintosh, were deeply interested in botany. Designs were taken from nature. Poppies, orchids, tulips and lilies were used extensively, and were often accompanied by heart-shaped leaves and curving whiplash tendrils. In the insect world, the dragonfly was favourite, while swans, snails and fish were also used decoratively.

Decorative menu holders in opaque glass. £50–£100 the pair.

The female figure was usually nude, although often depicted against a background [1] of flowing draperies. When clothed, the garments were loose yet clinging, giving the figure an air of sensuous abandonment.

Iridescent glass was produced by Tiffany (q.v.), Loetz and others. James Couper of Glasgow produced a cloudy glass of metallic appearance called Clutha, while Gallé and the Daum brothers were renowned for their carved and acid-etched cameo glass (q.v.). Lalique (q.v.) used an opalescent glass to great effect, with the patterns standing out in relief, and Eugene Rousseau experimented with crackle glass effects.

Colours were varied. For a landscape type of decoration, soft ambers, mid-browns and muted yellows could be used. Pastel shades of pink, blue and lavender gave a romantic background to carved and applied flowers such as the iris or daffodil. Iridescent glass was produced in both subdued rusts and browns and the vivid jewel-like colours of turquoise, and amethyst or violet.

Metal was often combined with the glass, and vases would sometimes be held in bronze, silver, plated, brass or pewter mounts which followed free-flowing open work designs.

RIGHT Wine glass with bell-shaped bowl and spiral rod stem, by James Powell, Whitefriars Glass Company c.1906/7. Height 8in; £40–£80.

LEFT Tazza in clear glass with a border of swagged threads in green glass and double air twist spiral stem by James Powell, Whitefriars Glass Company c.1906. Height 8in; £150–£200.

b

· BABY ·
· FEEDER ·
· BOTTLES ·

The practice of feeding a baby from a bottle has its roots in antiquity. In Greece, black terracotta bottles were used to feed the youngsters, while the Romans were the first to use glass. In the Middle Ages, mothers used polished cow horn feeders with leather teats but these were soon superseded by all leather and wooden bottles. Teats could be pieces of cloth or rag on which the baby would suck. Other materials were also used, such as parchment stuffed with sponge, fingers cut off gloves, and even pickled cows' udders were recommended. The first rubber teat appeared in 1845 when it was patented by Elijah Pratt in the USA.

Feeding bottles were made in china and earthenware, but these were largely replaced by glass bottles in 1832. As the interior of the bottle could be seen through the clear or aqua glass, it made for more hygienic cleaning.

In the 1880s, upright feeders were produced. An illustration from the Maws catalogue of that period shows that the bottles were fitted with a long rubber tube which ended in a teat.

'Allenbury's Feeder' bottle complete with box; £15–£25.

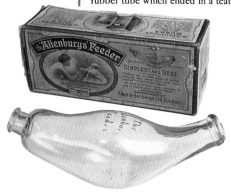

14

b

Known variously as the Fountain Feeding Bottle and the Alexandra Feeding Bottle, they came with a choice of stoppers. The buyer could choose caps or stoppers made of wood, earthenware or porcelain, metal or glass. The Alexandra was named after the then Princess of Wales, who later became Queen Alexandra.

In 1867, a Captain Webber took out a patent for a feeder which incorporated a thermometer but the idea did not catch on until about 1890 when Burroughs Wellcome & Co produced their Thermo-Safeguard feeding bottle.

Various shapes have been produced over the years but the most popular with mothers was the banana-shaped bottle which made its appearance in 1896. This was a double-ended bottle that was fitted with a teat and a screw-topped valve.

Avoid buying bottles that are chipped, cracked, or badly stained inside, unless they are rare. Dirty bottles respond well to soaking in dishwasher detergent (see also BOTTLES). If buying a Fountain Feeding Bottle, ensure that the tube is not perished and that the stoppers are in good condition.

The Thermo-Safeguard bottle originally cost one shilling and threepence (about 6½ pence), but collectors will now have to pay £75 or more for a good example. If the bottle is still in its original illustrated cardboard box, then the price will be even higher. The double-ended bottle manufactured by Maws was made in great quantity, and consequently these can be found for about £5–£15. The variation in price depends on the amount of embossing on the bottle. The teat is rarely with the bottle as this will have perished or been lost over the years.

b

· BASKETS ·

A great variety of glass baskets were made in the Stourbridge area during the late 19th and early 20th centuries and these can be found in all shapes and sizes. They could be functional and intended as cake or sweet baskets, match and spill holders, and posy holders, or they could be purely decorative and for ornamental or novelty use only.

The baskets were often little more than shallow pressed glass dishes (see PRESS-MOULDED GLASS) which had an all-over pattern. The glass handle was usually plain and would have been added while it was still slightly molten and malleable.

Small glass baskets often had a wickerwork pattern pressed into the glass. It is maintained that Sowerby's (q.v.) copied every basket and weave that had been used in the Victorian era. The Sowerby baskets were sometimes straight-sided, rather like log baskets. Taller examples would have been used as spill holders, shorter baskets were posy holders. Garden trugs held flowers. In addition to the 'woven' baskets, Sowerby's also used a portmanteau style for their baskets, and these were often made in their Malachite or New Marble Glass (see VITRO-PORCELAIN GLASS).

Novelty baskets were often made with pinched openings. The basket shape was pressed out by machine then, while the glass was still malleable, the sides were gently drawn or pinched together. The addition of handles made it impossible to use the basket for any practical purpose. These were produced in a variety of colours and effects, such as primrose and blue Pearline (q.v.), Malachite and Blanc-de-Lait, also made by Sowerby's.

Clear green glass basket with Sowerby trademark; £25–£35.

b

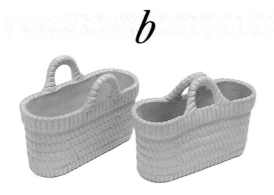

Delicate, clear glass baskets made in cranberry glass (q.v.) were a speciality of Thomas Webb (q.v.). These would stand on small out-curving feet in applied crystal. The clear glass handle would be ornamented with long leaf-like decorations where it joined the basket, and this decoration was continued on to the main body of the piece in frilled and trailing pinchwork and applied flowers. Sometimes the pink baskets were left plain, the only ornamentation being the delicately waved or frilled edges. These baskets were of larger size than those of the woven design made in pressed glass, and prices will range between £80 and £150 for a good example. The machine pressed baskets of about four inches (10 cm) in height will cost about £30 upwards, depending on the maker and the registration mark (see MAKERS' TRADEMARKS and REGISTERED DESIGN NUMBERS).

When buying, ensure that there are no cracks as damage will devalue the piece. Cracks are often difficult to see if the glass is of a detailed design or heavily ornamented, so check carefully. Check any frilled or trailed glass for chipping as this can be easily overlooked. Also check that the handle has not been repaired where it joins the basket.

Vitro-porcelain baskets with Sowerby trademark and date lozenge; £30–£45 each.

17

b

· BEADS ·

The Venetians first developed the art of glass bead making and, for centuries, their techniques were a closely guarded secret. The most sought after are the Chevron beads which were made from irregular canes of glass layered together to produce a multi-coloured bead in a corrugated 'chevron' pattern. Mosaic rod-shaped beads were made from fused glass canes which were then sliced and applied to a core of glass.

In the late 18th century, glassmakers in Bohemia (now Czechoslovakia) began manufacturing beads. They did not use the Venetian techniques but produced beads by methods such as blow-moulding (see BLOWN AND BLOW-MOULDED GLASS) and press-moulding (see PRESS-MOULDED GLASS). Artificial pearls were made by spraying the interior of the bead with 'essence d'orient', a substance produced from the scales of the bleak fish. This gave a pearly lustre to the blown glass. The beads would then be filled with wax to give them added weight.

Glass bead necklaces have retained their popularity over the years and can be found in long ropes or as shorter chokers. The Victorians made faceted black glass beads in imitation of jet; yellow glass was used in place of amber or natural stones, and clear glass simulated crystal. The holes in Victorian beads were often drilled by hand, and thus the opening is often irregular, sometimes having a flat, matt bevel around the edge. Holes of a precise, regular cut denote beads of a later period due to the introduction of mechanisation.

Early glass beads could be held together by fine wire hooks. These kept the beads apart and prevented rubbing.

Opalescent glass beads;
£10–£20 each.

Selection of glass beads;
£10–£20 each.

Occasionally a smaller bead was placed
in between the larger beads; sometimes
a slim disc of crystal, called a rondelle or
distance piece, was inserted. Silk thread
of a matching colour was used on small
beads, and this was firmly knotted
between each one. Cat gut or cord was
used for larger, heavier beads.

Coloured glass beads were sometimes
painted with tiny flower heads or in
swirling patterns. Silver and gold foiled
beads were made by placing a layer of
foil on to the basic bead before adding a
layer of clear glass. This produced a

bead which had a glittering textured appearance.

In the 1920s, there was renewed interest in beads and the fashion of the day dictated that they should reach well below the wearer's waist. These long ropes can be found at antiques fairs and markets and will cost from about £20.

When buying beads, it is important to check that the silk thread is not worn and that the knotting is not rubbed and fraying. The cost of restringing beads can be prohibitive, and a short necklace can cost in the region of £15–£20. It is possible to restring the beads oneself and kits can be bought at haberdashery counters, but it is difficult to obtain a tight, professional finish and, if the beads are valuable, it is better to approach an expert.

Check faceted beads for chipping, and ensure that painted glass beads are not cracked. Chain links should be firm and secure, although these are often easily repaired. Spring clasps should still operate under tension, and barrel clasps should be capable of being firmly screwed in place.

· BELLS ·

These novelties fall into the 'frigger' class (q.v.) and have been made in England since the 18th century. The output was at its greatest between about 1820 and 1850 when the demand for coloured glass was at its height. Sizes vary from a massive 17 inches (43 cm) diameter of the bell to those of 4 or 5 inches (22 cm).

The handle was sometimes of a contrasting colour, but was more often made of clear glass. Early examples have small handles, shorter than the height of the bell, and are of baluster shape, being knopped where they touch the bell. Air twist and cotton twist handles were made, the coloured threads of glass being twisted attractively in various patterns. Some handles had tear drop bubbles in them, while others had bands of red and blue in a 'barber's pole' style decoration.

Clappers were attached to the bell by loops or hooks of thin wire. This wire was fixed to the collar by embedding it firmly in plaster. The clappers could also be of coloured glass and they often terminated in a pear-shaped knob, although the knob could sometimes resemble a small clear glass marble.

The bell itself was infinitely varied. Clear glass examples were made in blue, red, pink, amber, amethyst and green. Opaque white bells were edged with red or blue glass, and sometimes concentric rings of white glass went a third of the way up ruby or cranberry bells. Latticinio twist bells were made in pale lemon, yellow, pink, white and blue. Nailsea style bells (see NAILSEA GLASS and NAILSEA-STYLE GLASS) were made with sectioned loops of red, blue and white, or would have combed wave patterns in red and blue on white. Occasionally the clear glass was of a twisted, rippled construction.

As bells are rarely found, it will not detract from their appeal if they are minus their clappers. If they do have the clapper, however, check that the plaster holding the wire is firm and not loose in any way. Prices will start at about £150–£200 for a plain coloured bell dating from around 1850.

Nailsea glass bell. 18th century; £150–£300.

· BISCUIT ·
· BARRELS ·

These containers were both decorative and functional and were extremely popular during the late Victorian era and

Frosted biscuit barrel with
silver-plated lid and
handle; £30–£45.

at the turn of the century. The fashion
for them saw a revival in the 1930s.

Every home had a sideboard or
chiffonier which contained the table
china, glass and cutlery, and on the
sideboard would be placed the biscuit
barrel. They were made in wood with
plated tops and a ceramic lining in china
or glass. Glass barrels would be cut
crystal, be moulded or pressed (see
PRESS-MOULDED GLASS) and some
extremely attractive examples can be
found. The most commonly found today
are those made of moulded glass in the
Chippendale pattern (see DAVIDSON,
GEORGE & CO), dating from the 1920s
and 1930s.

Victorian biscuit containers were
usually barrel-shaped and can be found
in cut glass, sometimes attractively
flashed with colour. The designs would
often be very ornate with fruit and/or
foliage contained within panels.

Edwardian barrels were also known as
biscuit boxes and sometimes had a
footed base. They were made in
pressed, moulded or cut glass and
designs would perhaps be of bold
diamond shapes, or perhaps have small
faceted diamonds cut into the glass.
Another form of popular decoration
would be to have sprays of fern
delicately etched into the glass. Again
lids could be of glass, although some of
the finer and better decorated barrels
would have lids of silver or EPNS
(Electro-Plated Nickel Silver).

One can find 1930s biscuit barrels
made in moulded glass and tending
towards a square shape. These often
have panels showing stylised Art Deco
designs such as birds or kneeling girls.
Brown or amber, blue, pink and green
were popular colours, and matching fruit
bowls were also made.

The handles on biscuit barrels varied

according to their lids. Silver-plated lids were accompanied by matching handles; glass-lidded barrels would either have no handles at all, or would have a handle made of woven wicker. This would be attached to the barrel by means of loops which fitted over glass projections on the barrel. If the handle is missing, it will detract from the value of the biscuit barrel, but will not necessarily make it less attractive.

Moulded glass biscuit barrels dating from about 1920 are widely available. The lids on these are almost always glass, and the inner lip of the lid and the rim of the biscuit barrel should be carefully checked for chipping when buying. They can be found for about £15 upwards. Those in pastel colours from the 1930s will be about £20–£30. Victorian biscuit barrels of cut glass, either clear or flashed, will cost between £90–£120.

When buying a biscuit barrel with a silver lid and handle, check that the metal is stamped with a full hallmark. This should include the assay office mark, the town mark, the standard mark, and a date letter. Silver-plated or EPNS lids should be of a good silver colour and not worn or yellowed. Check that the lid fits the barrel firmly and does not move about from side to side as it might with a replacement lid.

Amber moulded biscuit box c.1930; £15–£20.

The technique of blowing glass by mouth into a variety of shapes has been used in glass production for almost two thousand years. The long hollow blowing iron would be plunged into a container of molten glass (known as metal) to pick up a lump or gather of glass. The gather would then be rolled or marvered on to an iron slab. This cooling process gave the gather a slightly harder outer layer which would withstand the pressure of the blowing. The glassmaker would then blow vigorously down the tube while rotating the blowing iron to keep the molten metal in shape and manageable. The final form of the piece was attained by manipulating the plastic glass with various tools.

Blow-moulded glass was made by using roughly the same method, only this time the gather would be placed into a hinged mould before being blown. The pressure of blowing would force the glass against the mould, and it would then take on the pattern and/or shape of the mould. Moulded glass always bears a seam where the metal has forced its way into the slight gaps between the sections of the moulds. In blow-moulded glass, these are slight; in press-moulded glass (q.v.) the seams are more prominent. Sometimes the seams will have been fire polished to reduce them, but careful examination will usually reveal traces of the mould. After the blowing process the glass would then be placed into an annealing oven or lehr to be cooled slowly at a controlled rate.

Semi-automatic blow-moulded glass was made by putting the gather of glass into a parison mould which gave the glass its initial or embryo shape. The piece would then be transferred to a finishing mould where compressed air was applied to give the piece its final form.

Automatic glass blowing saw the initial gather of metal placed into the parison mould by machine. The process was then the same as for

Toilet bottle with female figure in Art Nouveau style c.1920. Height 5in; £20–£40.

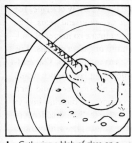

1 Gathering a blob of glass on a blowing iron.

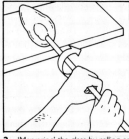

2 'Marvering' the glass by rolling on a smooth surface.

3 Blowing the glass into the required shape by mouth.

4 Shearing the top of the blown shape to the required height.

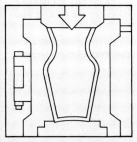

A Finished shape being blown in the blow mould.

B Finished article being taken out of the mould.

semi-automatic glass moulding, and the glass cooled in an annealing oven.

Because of the nature of the technique, blow-moulded glass always has the pattern on the outer surface, the inner surface being left smooth by the action of the blown or compressed air, unlike press-moulded glass which can have the pattern impressed into both surfaces.

Enamelled and gilt ruby glass urn and pedestal c.1850; £700–£1000.

· BOHEMIAN ·
· GLASS ·

The first half of the 19th century saw the glassmakers of Bohemia (now Czechoslovakia) experimenting with colours for glass and new, richer hues were produced. Hyalith glass was manufactured in about 1820. This was a yellow stained glass made in imitation of the semi-precious stone. Lithyalin was made a few years later and this glass closely resembled marble. It could be semi-transparent or opaque and was predominantly red in colour. A deep topaz yellow and later a rich ruby red were produced. This latter colour was achieved by adding copper to the molten glass; previously, real gold had been used which made the glass extremely costly. The addition of uranium saw the emergence of a new green in about 1830 which ranged between a clear vivid shade and a yellowish green. When ultramarine was added in varying quantities, it gave shades of blue ranging from a pale, delicate blue, to deep indigo.

To show off these new colours to advantage the Bohemian glass factories adopted the technique of flashing, casing and overlaying. One or more layers of white or coloured glass would be added to the piece of glass while still molten. This overlay or casing would then be cut away, often in complex patterns, to show the layer or layers beneath. Overlay usually refers to simple cutting patterns; the term cameo or cased is used when the glass was deeply engraved in relief or cameo fashion. Flashed glass was glass that had been stained or dipped in one colour only and then cut to reveal the clear glass beneath. Confusion can be caused, however, as on the Continent flashed

Perfume flask with gilded decoration c.1850; £150–£200.

glass is known as cased glass.

Early Bohemian glass is extremely expensive, and a single goblet can cost about £100–£150 upwards. It is therefore advisable to buy only from a reputable dealer.

· BOTTLES ·

Up until the early 19th century, earthenware containers had been popularly used in the sale of food and drink but some unscrupulous traders made a practice of adulterating the contents in order to make better profits (by mixing earth with cocoa, for example, or chalk and alum with flour and by adding dried leaves to tea, while beer was perked up with the addition of copperas and green vitriol). When the Victorians demanded that they should be able to see the contents before buying, the glass container came into its own.

Up until about 1845, glass bottles were made mainly in colours of green or brown. This was partly due to the manufacturers of soft drinks wanting to conceal the unsightly sediment that lay at the bottom of the bottle, and partly due to the high taxation levied on clear or flint glass. When these tax restrictions were finally lifted towards the middle of the 19th century, glass manufacturers began making clear glass containers, adding manganese to the mix to produce a colourless metal.

'Herb Beer' bottle with original label intact. Height 5in; £5–£10.

At first bottles were blow-moulded (see BLOWN AND BLOW-MOULDED GLASS) and were held on the pontil rod for support until the correct shape was achieved. After shearing the neck of the bottle, the base was broken off leaving an irregular lump of glass on the bottom. This gave an uneven base, and glassmakers soon adopted the technique

b

of pushing the pontil rod up into the bottle before breaking it off. This gave a characteristic deep indentation or 'kick-up'.

Bottles were later blown using hinged moulds, the neck and lip being added after the initial blowing. It was not until about 1898 that completely automatic bottle-making went into production. The characteristic seams that came with blow-moulding were largely eliminated in the mid-1800s by lining the inside of the mould with a smoothing compound. As the molten glass was turned in the mould, so any seams were smoothed out.

Mineral waters posed a problem due to the gaseous nature of their contents. William Hamilton produced an egg-shaped bottle in 1841. The odd shape made it practical to store the bottle on its side only, thus keeping the cork moist and swollen and preventing it from blowing out. In 1872, Hiram Codd patented a mineral water bottle which

Various mineral water and beer bottles; £3–£8.

had a built-in glass stopper. This marble-like stopper was held in the neck of the bottle by two glass lugs. Any gas that formed forced the marble hard against the rubber seal in the neck. A wooden cap and plunger was supplied with each bottle, enabling the user to press the stopper down for ease of pouring.

The development of the use of brass castings in the making of bottles enabled manufacturers to emboss the bottles. This meant that the advertising of the contents could be done cheaply and attractively, and by the late 1800s 75 per cent of all bottles were embossed.

This embossing ranged between the simple marking of bottles such as Bovril or Lea & Perrins, and the ornate cartouches and insignias of companies such as H. H. Warner of New York. This enterprising manufacturer of patent medicines had his bottles

b

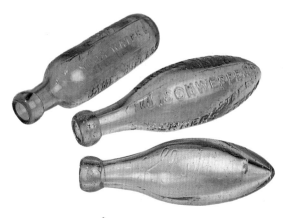

Mineral water bottles
including two Hamilton
bottles £3–£6 each.

ornamented with a heavily embossed
safe, using the symbol as a play on
words to underline the quality of his
product.

However, the method of turn-
moulding that produced bottles with a
smoother outer surface led to the use of
labels being stuck on the bottles and in
about 1870 when this was done by
machine the embossing of bottles went
into a decline.

Most of the various bottles found for
sale today are those rescued from the
Victorian rubbish dumps of years past
and consequently they can be badly
marked. Some bottles achieve an
attractive iridescence by being buried
for a prolonged period but, as washing
will remove this, it might be best left
alone. Some stains can be impossible to
remove, although surface dirt will
respond well to overnight soaking in a
biological or dishwasher detergent.
Internal staining can be dealt with by
putting a little gravel and water into the
bottle and shaking vigorously. Rust
stains will respond to this treatment if
they have first been treated with rust
remover.

If buying a rare specimen or a bottle

that is ornately embossed, some internal staining can be tolerated but, in general, it is best to go for clean bottles which can generally be found at antiques fairs and markets and at boot sales. There are also several regular bottle fairs and collectors' fairs which provide the enthusiast with a rich hunting ground. It is impossible to give an indication of price as there is such a wide variety of bottles available. Generally, mineral water bottles can be purchased for about 50 pence each, but rare 'Crown' bottles will cost anything from about £40–£50 upwards, and there are some bottles that are even more expensive.

Bottle collecting is very much a specialised subject and further reading is essential, as is touring around antiques markets and bottle fairs to get the 'feel' of the subject (see also BABY FEEDER BOTTLES; COMMERCIAL PERFUME BOTTLES; MEDICINE & POISON BOTTLES; and SCENT BOTTLES).

Codd-style mineral water bottles; £5–£15.

· BRIERLEY · · CRYSTAL ·

See *Stevens & Williams*

· BRISTOL · · GLASS ·

The discovery of cobalt oxide (known as smalt) in Saxony in the mid-18th century led to its being used in glass making. It was extremely expensive to import, however, and the search began for cobalt deposits in Britain. A small amount was discovered in Cornwall, and the rights to this mine were later sold to William Cooksworthy of Bristol.

The Bristol glassmakers used the cobalt to great effect, producing a glass of an intense dark blue. However,

b

glassmakers all over England soon began production and the term 'Bristol glass' therefore has to be regarded as generic rather than referring to the exact area of manufacture. Colours other than blue were also produced, such as a deep, brilliant green, a delicate amethyst, and a more rare yellow, and dark ruby red.

Although there were more than a dozen glassmakers operating in the Bristol area during the 18th century, the most well known was Isaac Jacobs. He owned the Non-Such Flint Glass Manufactory, and some of his products are marked I. Jacobs. A favourite motif of the day was the gilded Greek key design and this was used on goblets, finger bowls, plates and other tableware.

Other techniques of ornamentation were cold-painting and enamelling. Fruit and flowers in colours of red and blue would adorn wine glasses and pickle jars. Gilding enhanced the dark blue glass, and decanters with their pear-shaped stoppers were decorated with vine leaves, bunches of grapes, and scrolls. The name of the contents of the decanter, such as claret, brandy, hock, port or rum, would be added in gilt lettering, sometimes enclosed in an elaborate cartouche. These decanters were also made in the distinctive green glass.

Blue finger bowl with anthemion design in gilt c.1825. Height 3¼in; £500–£600.

Blue onion-shaped carafe engraved with mistletoe band c.1840. Height 8½in; £200–£250.

b

Cruets were copied in decanter shapes and were contained within plated holders. These were decorated in a similar fashion to the decanters.

Michael Edkins was perhaps the best-known decorator of the Bristol area and is first mentioned in the record books in 1763, when his stock book shows he charged two shillings for gilding a set of four blue jars and beakers with a mosaic border.

The Nailsea Glasshouse (see NAILSEA GLASS and NAILSEA-STYLE GLASS) which was situated just outside Bristol was initially known for its pale green window glass (q.v.).

Late 18th-century Bristol glass is rare and prohibitively priced but later wine glasses in the same rich colours can be readily found and will cost about £30–£50 each. It is possible to build these up into sets of matching or harlequin colours. A small carafe made in green glass in about 1860 will cost about £150–£200.

Amethyst cream jug with flared lip and looped handle c.1820. Height 3¾in; £180–£250.

· BULB · VASES ·
See Hyacinth Vases

· BURMESE · · GLASS ·

This dates from about 1885 when the first patent was taken out in America by Frederick Shirley. It went into production in 1886 at the Mount Washington Glass Company in New Bedford, Massachusetts, and in the same year Thomas Webb (q.v.) acquired the manufacturing rights in England.

Burmese glass is a soft yellow colour with pink under- or overtones. The colour was achieved by the addition of gold and uranium to the ingredients.

The uranium produced an opaque yellow which when reheated gave a partial shading of blush pink. It is said that Queen Victoria was so impressed by the new American glass when she saw it, that Thomas Webb named his version of it in her honour, calling it 'Queen's Burmese'. Webb's early pieces are marked 'Queen's Burmese Thomas Webb & Sons, Patent' on an impressed disc. Also shown is the registration number 56,664 (see REGISTERED DESIGN NUMBERS). Webb later altered the 'recipe' for his glass and produced a richer colour.

Lampshade by Webb with painted acorn decoration c.1880; £200–£400.

Other manufacturers made similar glass and sold it under various trade names, such as Amberina (amber/ruby), Alexandrite (blue/purplish red), and Sunrise, which was similar to Webb's Queen's Burmese but less subtle.

Burmese glass was mainly used for ornamental pieces such as vases, posy holders, sweetmeat and other small dishes. Table centrepieces were also made and these could consist of several small vases held by metal supports, standing on a mirrored base. In America, the glass proved popular and Samuel Clarke used it in the manufacture of his 'Fairy' Lamps (q.v.).

Burmese glass is expensive to buy. For example, a Webb vase made in about 1888 and about four inches (10 cm) in height will cost £250 or more. Buyers should also beware of reproduction Burmese glass. This has been produced in both Italy and America since the 1950s. The colours have a harder appearance to them and comparison with an original piece will soon show up the differences, but the inexperienced collector could easily make a mistake. It is therefore best to buy from a reputable dealer who will guide and advise.

C

· CAMEO · GLASS ·

Although the carving of cased glass in a relief or cameo technique came into prominence in the late 1800s, cameo glass had been produced in Rome as long ago as the 1st century BC. Wheel engraved cameo work had been carried out in Europe in the 17th and 18th centuries, and the Chinese manufactured beautifully decorated snuff bottles in the 18th century. But it was not until about 1870 that cameo glass was made in any great quantity in England.

The most famous example of cameo glass is the Portland Vase, now in the British Museum. This vase was made in the 1st century AD, and has dark blue glass overlaid with a layer of white. The carvings are of classical figures and are thought to represent those of Peleus and Thetis at their wedding. The vase was found in a Roman sarcophagus and the first mention of it is in 1626 when it passed into the hands of the Barberini family. Known then as the Barberini Vase, it was brought to England in 1784 and purchased a year later by Lady Portland. The firm of Josiah Wedgwood copied the vase in Jasperware in 1786, and when the original vase was later smashed by a madman, it was pieced together using this vase as a copy.

Scent bottle in grey and yellow glass overlaid with red and decorated with ferns and having a green glass stopper c.1900. Signed Gallé. £1000+.

C

Cameo glass pilgrim flask in amber overlay with dragonfly and lily pond decoration c.1900. Signed Gallé. Height 3in; £500–£700.

Ovoid vase in white glass cased with sapphire blue and decorated with a thistle design c.1890. Signed Gallé. Height 6¾in; £1000+.

This wanton damage brought the vase to public notice once more, and glassmakers became interested in the technique of cameo carving. John Northwood (q.v.) first produced the Elgin Vase which was carved on a single layer of clear glass. He then produced a copy of the Portland Vase in about 1877, although this suffered a crack shortly after manufacture.

Thomas Webb's factory (q.v.) is also associated with cameo work and produced the Rose Vase which was carved on two layers of glass in about 1885. George and Thomas Woodall were Webb's two most famous artists in the field of cameo carving and their work is highly prized. Later, Webb's produced cameo work which was engraved on to three layers of glass. Stevens & Williams (q.v.) of Brierley Hill were also well known for their cameo work.

English designs were usually on a classical theme. Where flowers and/or foliage were used, these were botanically correct and accurately represented.

On the Continent, Gallé (q.v.) became renowned for his superb cameo work. He first showed his glass at the Paris Exhibition in 1889. Gallé favoured free-form artistry and his designs are less restrained than those of the English factories. He portrayed insects such as dragonflies and butterflies, leaves and flowers, and even engraved landscapes in delicate relief.

Up until about 1880, cameo glass was carved by hand, great care being taken painstakingly to cut away the glass in shallow layers. This gave a realistic three-dimensional effect. From about 1880–90, however, glassmakers used the copper wheel, and hydrofluoric acid was used on large areas. After this date, acid was more widely used to eat away the unwanted glass, and the standard of cameo work declined, with designs becoming flatter and more shallow.

Signed glass by Webb or Gallé is extremely expensive and a seven-inch (17 cm) cameo vase in five colours made by Thomas Webb will cost from £2500 or more. Later, unsigned cameo work can be found for about £80–£100 upwards, but it is best to buy from a reputable dealer who will guide and advise.

· CANDLESTICKS ·

Glass candlesticks have been used since the early 16th century. The majority were imported into Britain from Venice but in about 1742 a London glassmaker advertised his diamond-cut glass candlesticks. Regency candlesticks were made of lead crystal and cut and faceted for added sparkle. The early Victorian era saw candlesticks mass-produced in moulded and pressed glass (see BLOWN AND BLOW-MOULDED GLASS, and PRESS-MOULDED GLASS) which made it possible for the poorest householder to have his home attractively illuminated. Nightlights were placed in pretty glass containers, such as the Fairy Lamp (q.v.) patented by Samuel Clarke, and were used in the bedroom.

Early examples followed the style of brass candlesticks and were cut into knopped baluster shapes. They rarely had a drip pan, relying on the wide turned-over neck to form a collar and catch the tallow drips.

The majority of glass candlesticks were of single, columned form set on a wider base. Some of these were columnar, or vase or goblet-shaped, and were lavishly decorated with long faceted glass drops or lustres (q.v.)

Candlestick with wrythen socket and double series opaque twist stem, with domed and moulded foot c.1760. Height 8in; £800–£1200.

C

Clear glass candle and chambersticks, 20th century.
LEFT TO RIGHT: £10–£15 for a pair; £5–£8; £18–£25.

One of a pair of pressed glass candlesticks in 'oily' green glass c.1900. £20–£30 the pair.

which caught the light. The sticks were usually sold in pairs and would stand either side of the mantelpiece. Candlesticks were also included as part of a trinket set (q.v.) which stood on the dressing table in the bedroom.

Late Victorian candlesticks were made in both clear and coloured glass. Stourbridge manufacturers produced blue, red, green and amber, with a particularly vivid oily yellow/green being quite common. The latter can sometimes be mistakenly called Vaseline glass (q.v.) so care should be taken when buying as Vaseline glass is considerably more collectable.

In the 1920s and 1930s, pink, green and blue candlesticks were made in the style of the day. Female figures often formed the stem, a mermaid being most popular. Cloud glass (q.v.) manufactured by Davidson (q.v.) in 1922 was made in brown and amber, red (rare), purple, blue, grey (rare) and green.

Because pressed glass was cheap and plentiful, it is not difficult to find single candlesticks in clear glass for about £8–£10. A pair of oily yellow sticks will be about £25–£40, and a squat cloud glass candlestick in red about two-and-a-half inches (6 cm) high will cost about £45–£5

When buying, check the collar and holder for chips, and examine any ornate pressed glass specimens for cracks which might be hidden in the pattern. Ensure that any lustres which might be present are all matching and not chipped in any way.

· CARNIVAL · · GLASS ·

In the late 1800s, art glass was all the rage, particularly the shimmering iridescent glass produced by Tiffany (q.v.) in America. By 1886, the process of iridising glass was well known and Tiffany's patent was not renewed. This opened the way for American glass manufacturers to copy the process, but it was not until 1907–8 that the Fenton Glassware Company of West Virginia produced the first piece of what is now known as Carnival glass.

The glass was originally called fanciful names, such as 'Taffeta' and 'Aurora' glass, 'New Venetian', 'Venetian Art', 'Etruscan' and 'Rainbow'. It was referred to as 'Poor man's Tiffany' and was derided as being gaudy. Within the trade it was called simply 'iridised pressed glassware' (see PRESS-MOULDED GLASS). It received the rather puzzling name of Carnival glass in the early to mid-1900s when a great

Marigold Dugan banana boat in 'Peach and Pear' pattern; £70–£150.

C

BACK ROW: Marigold decanter, 'Golden Harvest' pattern. £100–£150 (with set of matching glasses £200–£250).
Green Fenton vase 'Diamond Rib' pattern £12–£20.
FRONT ROW: Marigold cup and saucer in 'Kittens' pattern, part of a child's teaset. £120–£150 for cup and saucer.

deal of inferior glass was sold to the owners of amusement arcades and funfairs to be offered as prizes on the stalls.

There were five major manufacturers of Carnival glass in America: the Fenton Glassware Company, the Imperial Glass Company of Ohio, the Millersburg Glass Company, also in Ohio, the Northwood Glass Company in West Virginia, and the Dugan-Diamond Works in Pennsylvania.

In England, the manufacturers were Sowerby's (q.v.), George Davidson & Co (q.v.) and Henry Greener & Co (q.v.)

Production of Carnival glass tailed off in the 1920s as the demand for it fell. Secondary quality glass was still being produced in Australia, Europe and Scandinavia between about 1923 and 1939, and pieces made by Eda Glasbruks in Sweden are of extremely

LEFT: Amber stemmed bowl by Imperial in 'Grape' pattern; £40–£60 *RIGHT*: Red fluted bowl by Fenton in 'Holly' pattern; £200–£450. (In Marigold only £20–£30.)

40

fine quality.

Carnival glass was made by press-moulding (see PRESS-MOULDED GLASS) and after the initial firing the coloured glass was coated with a mixture of metallic salts (different salts gave different effects). The glass was then fired again to 'set' the iridescence. The addition of this iridescence could appear to alter the colour of the piece and, sometimes, only by holding it up to the light can the true or base colour be seen. This colour is strongest at the rim or base of the glass item.

The most commonly seen colour is marigold, and this ranges from a vivid flame-like shade to a pale orange. Other colours are green (various shades), cobalt blue, amethyst (unusual), purple, and red (rare and highly prized). There are pale variations on these colours, and all are desirable.

Carnival glass was made in various shapes and designs. The glassware was intended to be utilitarian and a variety of items were made: fruit and salad bowls, sugar and cream sets, butter dishes, dessert sets, carafes and beakers, punch bowls and cups, vases (all shapes and sizes), celery vases, comports and tazzas, plates (large and small), hatpin holders and trinket pots, and shallow dishes. The latter are often seen at antiques fairs and the variety to be found is enormous.

As Carnival glass was still very malleable when it left the mould, the edges were pulled into various shapes: flutes, ruffles, crimps and pleats, for example. These edges were often quite intricately patterned and care needs to be taken when buying such pieces as a rim chip can often be overlooked. It is best to run a finger all around the edge, preferably with eyes closed, to ensure that there is no damage.

Blue rose bowl by Northwood in 'Leaf and Beads' pattern; £45–£75.

C

The designs pressed into the plates are also infinitely varied, and often a manufacturer can be recognised from the pattern used, although many glassmakers did, in fact, copy each other. For examples, 'Grape and Cable' and 'Peacock and Urn' were made by several factories. Some of the designs show Oriental influences, such as 'Dragon and Lotus' (Fenton) and 'Nippon', a series of scallops, the idea taken from a Japanese design book by Northwood. The peacock was also an influence as in 'Peacock and Urn', 'Peacock' (Northwood), 'Peacock Tail' (Fenton), 'Peacock at the Fountain' (Northwood) and 'Heart and Vine' which despite its name features stylised peacock feathers.

Flowers, fruit and foliage were used extensively by all manufacturers and one can find 'Wreath of Roses' (Fenton, and Dugan), 'Iris' (Fenton), 'Raspberry' (Northwood), 'Acorns' and 'Dandelion' (Fenton), 'Maple Leaf' (Dugan), 'Rose Show' (Northwood) and 'Wishbone' (Northwood). The latter is oddly named, since the pattern shows a stylised orchid. However, the patterns are immensely diverse and one can find all sorts of motifs from a Dutch Windmill ('Double Dutch' by Imperial) to a horse's head ('Pony' attributed to Dugan).

LEFT: Green footed plate by Fenton in 'Peacock and Grape' pattern; £35–£75. RIGHT: Purple plate by Imperial in 'Scroll Emboss' pattern; £65–£95.

There is such a variety of colours and designs in Carnival glass that it can bewilder the beginner and it is best to visit antiques fairs and markets and become familiar with the glass before buying in earnest. Carnival glass was reproduced in the 1950s, mostly in marigold, but now excellent copies are coming from (it is thought) Taiwan. These are stamped N and can be mistaken for Northwood pieces. So far, three patterns have been identified: 'Good Luck', 'Grapes Vintage' and 'Peacock on the Fence'. They are excellent copies, but are heavier than the original glass and have a rather leaden look and feel to them.

Prices vary enormously according to the colour and/or design of the piece. A shallow bowl in marigold with a scalloped edge and shallow crimps will cost about £25–£30; a sugar bowl in marigold can be found for about £10–£15; a punch bowl on stand will be about £65–£100; and a purple dish with 'Pansy' decoration by Imperial will be about £45–£60.

· CASED · GLASS ·
See Cameo Glass

· CELERY · VASE ·
The Victorians were extremely innovative and manufactured goods for every conceivable household purpose. Large two- or three-pronged forks were used for passing bread around the table; a whole range of nutpicks were designed to cope with every variety of nut; and gadgets of every kind abounded in the kitchen.

No self-respecting hostess would think the tea table complete without a handsome cut glass (see CUTTING,

GLASS) celery vase. These flared glass containers are often mistaken for flower vases and can, indeed, be used for this purpose. Some are footed, resembling an enormous wine goblet, and the height varies between seven inches (17 cm) for an unfooted version, to ten inches (25 cm) for a vase with a wine glass style foot.

With the advent of pressed glass (see PRESS-MOULDED GLASS) in the late 1800s, celery vases were made in a great variety of patterns. This gives the collector great scope, for some of the plainer vases and those of moulded (see BLOWN AND BLOW-MOULDED GLASS) rather than pressed glass can be found for about £10–£20.

The pressed glass patterns are sharper and more incisive than those produced by moulding, and can often be mistaken for cut glass. However, cut glass will be considerably dearer so it is worth checking carefully before buying. Hand-cut glass often shows tiny irregularities in the cutting, whereas pressed glass is of a uniform pattern.

Every major manufacturer in the Stourbridge area produced celery vases and these are often marked with the manufacturer's name (see MAKERS' TRADEMARKS), and/or a registered number or diamond (see REGISTERED DESIGN NUMBERS), making it possible to identify the maker and the date of manufacture.

Celeries, as they were known in the glass trade, are usually found in clear glass, although an advertisement by Sowerby (q.v.) for 1880 shows that he produced them in his 'Ivory' opaque glass; Davidson's (q.v.) produced them in brown marble vitro-porcelain (q.v.), suitably pressed in neo-classical style; Molineaux Webb designed celery vases with a clear Greek key design set

Cut glass celery vase with fan cut rim, and diamond and flute cut body c.1810. Height 8in; £150–£300.

against an opaque frosted finish. This design was registered in 1864, and the part-frosted patterns soon became popular. The firm also manufactured 'Duchess', a sharply-pressed pattern that was made in imitation of cut glass.

Clear pressed glass vases will cost about £25–£40; those of coloured pressed glass will be about £80–£100 upwards depending on the pattern. Plain celery vases enhanced with wheel engraving will cost about £50–£80, and those of cut glass will be about £80–£120 upwards.

· CHANDELIERS ·

In the Middle Ages, chandeliers were made in wood, metal and gesso (a type of plaster) and it was not until the 18th century that they were made in glass. These were first made in Venice, when the bronze base was decorated with ornamental glass flowers and leaves.

As the demand for chandeliers grew, three basic styles gradually evolved: antique, Adam and Regency. These styles were little changed during the early Victorian era, despite the introduction of gas lighting. It was not until the electric light bulb made its appearance later in the century that

LEFT: Flute and diamond cut vase with trumpet bowl and star cut foot c.1820. Height 10in; £150–£300.

RIGHT: Oval cut celery vase with scalloped edge and plain foot. Early 19th century. Height 9in; £50–£70.

modifications were made.

Early chandeliers were of a simple design which had a central shaft of cut glass spheres or balls which supported long curved 'S'-shaped arms that resembled tubes of plain glass. This style was later followed by chandeliers which were garlanded and festooned with delicate loops of crystal in faceted pear- or tear-shapes. As the century progressed, so the drops became more deeply cut and the number of branches increased. These gave an airy appearance to the chandelier. As an alternative, the chandelier could appear almost like a solid column of scintillating glass that reached up to the ceiling. The glass 'chains' led down to various tiers of rule cut drops or lustres (q.v.) and were so tightly wired together that the candles reflected a blaze of light.

When gas was introduced into homes in the 1830s, the gas pipes were incorporated into the chandelier and the slender glass branches gave way to those made of metal. Glass arms were later reintroduced with the advent of electricity, but the amount of metal in the chandelier was gradually increased, thus phasing out the glittering cascade of light.

· CHEESE · · DISHES ·

These household objects were originally made in pottery, but with the advent of pressed and moulded glass (see BLOWN AND BLOW-MOULDED GLASS and PRESS-MOULDED GLASS) in the late 19th century, glass cheese dishes were made in great quantity.

These were manufactured in the traditional shape, with a wedge-shaped cover set on a rectangular base. Patterns were simple, the glass being moulded into a reeded or shallow scalloped design. Apart from being made in clear glass, the dishes can also be seen in amber, and later 1930s examples were produced in blue, pink and green. Clear glass examples are easily found in antiques fairs and will cost from about £5 upwards. An amber-coloured cheese dish from the turn of the century with a leaf-shaped design on the cover and a large faceted knob will cost about £15.

When buying, check for cracks and/or chips. Check also that the cover sits firmly on the base and that it does not move around too much, which it will do if the two pieces are a marriage and not original.

Glass domes set on circular wooden bases are attractive, but these are not antiques and therefore of no antique value.

· CHIPPENDALE · · GLASS ·

See Davidson, George & Co,
and Cloud Glass

· CHRISTMAS · · TREE · · DECORATIONS ·

In the mid-1800s, Prince Albert, the Prince Consort, introduced the Christmas tree to his young family. The fashion caught on, and decorated pine trees became part of the British way of life.

At first, decorations consisted of gilded and painted pine cones and nuts, sweets, toys and gifts, and it was not until about 1860 that the first glass baubles appeared. Like the idea of the tree, these came from Germany, and the best were made in the village of

Large 'witch ball' style decorations once used on Queen Victoria's tree at Osborne House; £50–£80 each.

Lauscha in Thuringia. There were a great many small local glasshouses here and the manufacture of baubles developed from the practice of making small blown-glass beads (q.v.) in the late 18th century. At first, these coloured glass baubles were large and heavy and had cork stoppers with wires for hanging. Later, smaller baubles were finished with small glass hooks for attachment to the tree. After about 1880, however, the glass ball was sheared off at the neck and a cap of metal such as tin was fitted. A flat, and later, a round wire hook was used for hanging the ball on to the tree. After about 1918, these caps were often brassed or gilded.

The glass balls were often decoratively gilded and/or sprayed with lacquer. Gelatine was used as a fixing agent and gold or silver dust was sprinkled on to them to give added glitter. Fruit was painted on in oils, with fabric leaves added for a realistic effect. A dark silver finish was achieved on plain glass balls by coating the interior with a liquid lead solution; if the lead solution ran unevenly, then a layer of coloured wax was poured into the ball, thus producing an attractive variegated pattern. A mirror finish was produced by the use of silver nitrate.

C

Icicles were made by twisting delicate glass rods, but these were fragile and are rarely seen today.

As the demand for decorations grew, the glass blowers began using carved wooden moulds for their glass blowing (see BLOWN AND BLOW-MOULDED GLASS) and baubles in the shape of birds, fruit, pine cones, bells and angels were produced. These were painted and gilded decoratively. Bells would sometimes have tiny clappers. The birds would often have spun glass tails which fanned out attractively, and they were attached to the tree by metal clips which fitted on to springs on the bird's body. The slightest draught made the ornaments sway and glitter prettily. Early moulded baubles show irregularities, later plaster moulds produced baubles of a more regular shape.

By the 1920s, glass Christmas tree decorations were being mass-produced in both America and Japan, and the German monopoly was lost. Designs now included miniature horns and trumpets which could be blown to produce a noise, and as these were given to children to play with, they are very rare.

Early glass ornaments are difficult to

LEFT: White globe with cut-out transfer decoration c.1860; £50–£70
RIGHT: Globe with splashed colour c.1860; £40–£60.

find because of their fragility, and one can expect to pay £50 upwards for a well-decorated piece. Check that the sheared-off neck is undamaged and that the metal cap and hanger are original – glass ornaments made nowadays are of similar shape and design to those made in the 1930s and 1950s but modern caps and fittings are of a brighter metal. As birds were so popular with the Victorians and made in large numbers, these are most often found and will cost about £10–£15. Check that the spun glass tails and the painted body are in good condition. (See also FAIRY LIGHTS.)

· CIGAR · · HOLDERS ·

Cigars have been smoked in Europe since about 1650, but the fashion did not reach England until about 1815 when import restrictions were lifted. Cigar holders (also known in the early days as tubes) were made in a variety of materials: metal, wood, ceramic, natural stones (such as jet, cornelian or onyx), ivory, tortoiseshell, gutta-percha (a type of latex), vulcanite (an early plastic), meerschaum (a type of clay), amber and glass.

Attribution of the glass cigar and cheroot holders of the 19th century is difficult. Many resemble the Nailsea-type glass ornaments produced in the Stourbridge area (see NAILSEA GLASS, and NAILSEA-STYLE GLASS); others are similar to the type of work carried out in the Bohemian (q.v.) glasshouses.

The cigar holder shape is tube-like, wide at one end, tapering to a round or flat-lipped mouthpiece. Sizes vary between just under three inches (7 cm) to over six inches (15 cm), and the widest 'bowl' is about three-quarters of an inch (1 cm).

The variety of design was considerable. Gaily striped 'barber pole' effects were achieved by using differently coloured glass rods twisted into a spiral. Cut glass specimens include those in made coloured glass, where curved facets and diamonds added interest to the plain glass. Overlaid and flashed glass was used to great effect (see CAMEO GLASS), and patterns include geometric designs of circles, crosses and diamonds as well as stylised sprays of foliage and/or flowers. Various colours were used in the layers, pink, blue, red and opaque white, for example, but there were seldom more than three layers used.

Clear glass was coloured in ruby red, pink (see CRANBERRY GLASS), blue, green, yellow, and brown.

Cigar holders are not often seen at antiques fairs and markets as many dealers do not recognise them for what they are. For buying, it is best to approach a specialist dealer. Prices will range between about £35 and £45 for clear glass, but those in cased glass will cost almost double.

· CLARET · JUGS ·

In the mid-19th century the duty on claret wine was removed which revived the wine's popularity and it became a drink often served at the dinner table. As it was a wine that needed to be decanted to remove the unwanted sediment and to allow it to 'breathe', the claret jug soon made its appearance.

These tall jugs were made in metal or glass, and glass examples were often metal-mounted, having handles, attached lids and collars in silver, silver-gilt, pewter, spelter or plated metal. The Victorians often had their claret

Jug with engraved fern decoration c.1850; £100–£150.

C

An Art Nouveau W.M.F. green claret jug with pierced stopper and pewter mounts showing the faces of two maidens at the base and having a stylised tree handle. Height 14½in; £700–£900.

warm (at room temperature) and sometimes it was heated. As the heat would crack the glass handle, this was replaced by one of metal.

The shape varied between a tapering jug with a wide base, to an urn-like ewer. The metal handles were often extremely ornate and sometimes curved around the body of the jug in a Bacchanalian pattern of vine leaves and grapes. Where it joined the jug, the handle might be ornately scrolled. Sometimes the 'shoulders' of the jug were encased in metal and this could consist of ornamental panels or leaf shapes. Art Nouveau jugs (see ART NOUVEAU GLASS) had widely flared bases and were set within a 'cage' of metal that swirled artistically around the jug and up to the collar and lid. The height of claret jugs varied between about eight and fifteen inches (20–38 cm).

Clear glass jugs could be etched or cut, and a hobnail-cut pattern was popular. Flowers and leaves (other than vines) also decorated the jug. Frosted glass was used in conjunction with ornate metal work, the latter enhancing

Claret jug with cut mushroom stopper. Diamond and flute cutting and feather-cut strap handle c.1820. Height 8in; £500–£700.

C

Large claret jug with prismatic cutting, strap handle and star cut foot c.1810. Height 12in; £700–£900.

the cool clarity of the frosting. The Art Nouveau period saw dark green or cranberry glass (q.v.) being used to great effect, and contrasting well with the dark grey colour of the pewter or spelter mounts.

Claret jugs are not cheap and a good example will cost about £500 upwards. A small jug with a hobnail-cut pattern will be about £150–£300. It is important to check this type carefully as chips do not show up on the complex pattern and can be easily missed. An Art Nouveau jug with the metal casing made by WMF (Wurtenberg Metal Fabriken) will cost anything between about £700 and £900, depending on the design. It is possible to buy more cheaply at auction than from a specialist dealer but careful viewing is recommended. If paying a great deal of money for the decanter, it is advisable to buy from a reputable dealer who will make certain that there is no damage. A jug by WMF could occasionally have a replacement glass inner and this is permissible (providing the price is right: £100–£150) as these jugs are prized more for their metal work than for the glass interior.

C

· CLOUD · GLASS ·

This attractively streaked glass was made by George Davidson (q.v.) between about 1922 and 1940. After Davidson's success with the invention and patenting of the flower block – a solid dome of glass that was pierced to take the stalks of blooms – in 1910, trade began to fall off. There was a recession in the glass trade after World War I, and this was further exacerbated by the competition of cheap glass from abroad. In an effort to regain a share of the market, Davidson's began making non-utilitarian items and the success of the flower block led to the manufacture of vases, posy holders and bowls.

It was discovered that by introducing a quantity of dark metal (glass) into amber glass while it was still molten and before pressing (see PRESS-MOULDED GLASS), the darker glass trailed in cloud-like threads through the amber. This new glass was mentioned in the 'Pottery Gazette' in 1923 and received approval. The first colours to be produced were amber and purple, with unstreaked blue, green and black items being made from the same moulds. The glass, both streaked and plain, had one polished and one matt surface, the matt finish being achieved by acid etching. Blue Cloud Glass was introduced in 1925, tortoiseshell in 1928. This was similar to amber but more transparent.

Red Cloud Glass was not introduced until 1930 and this is the rarest colour to be found. The 'Pottery Gazette' described it as 'brilliant scarlet networked in black'. Emerald green was added to the range in 1933, jade green having been added to the plain glass range in 1931.

In 1933, Davidson's acquired the moulds and trade marks of Chippendale

Large platter in amethyst and purple. Diameter 11¼in; £15–£25.

Glass from the National Glass Company, and used the new moulds to produce an even wider range of Cloud Glass. Items were now being made such as bathroom sets, dressing table sets (consisting of a large tray, powder bowls, trinket pots, pin tray and ring holder), vases, fruit bowls, salad bowls and servers, flower bowls (with or without stands and/or flower blocks), jugs and beakers, candlesticks and table lamps, sundae dishes, and ashtrays. The range was enormous with over 100 moulds being used in ten different colourways. 'Modified orange' had made its appearance around 1934, and this was streaked with white. It is believed that there were some items made in a streaked grey, but it is unclear when this rare colour was introduced.

Up until recently Cloud Glass has been largely overlooked by collectors of glass, and even now it can be bought relatively cheaply. A trinket pot or powder bowl in blue will cost about £15–£20; in red, however, it will be about £75–£85. A vase of a typically tapered shape in amber will be about £25–£35; a purple flower bowl about nine inches (22 cm) in diameter, with a flower dome, will cost about £35–£45.

LEFT: Small bowl on stand in green with purple/amethyst streaking; £15–£20.
RIGHT: Large trinket pot in brown glass; £10–£20.

· COCKTAIL ·
· GLASSES ·
· & · SHAKERS ·

During the 1920s, entertaining one's friends for late afternoon or early evening cocktails became the 'done' thing, and the fashion continued through the 1930s. Large hotels such as the Ritz served champagne cocktails, and small cocktail bars became de rigueur in the homes of the wealthy. As the 1920s moved into the 30s, the Art Deco (q.v.) style took over and home cocktail bars became extremely stylised. Geometric lines and curves emphasised the 'Odeon' style of the cabinets and the interiors were lavishly mirrored and chromed.

Glassware followed the same design and cocktail shakers were made in glass, chrome or in a combination of both. Shakers were tall and cylindrical and had a cap that secured the ingredients when mixing or shaking and an inner strainer that neatly sieved the fruit

20th century shaker, engraved and enamelled; £20–£25.

content when pouring out the drink. Some shakers were made as jugs, the contents being stirred by means of a pair of revolving paddles.

The glasses were generally stemmed, the bowl flaring out conically. The clear glass bowls would have coloured stems and feet in bold colours, green, red, or black, perhaps. Or the whole glass would be decorated with concentric rings and/or bands of colour such as red, yellow, mint green, black, gold or silver. Favourite colour combinations were red and black and these were often paired for dramatic effect.

Frosting was also used a great deal as a decorative feature and this either covered the whole piece, etched on to the glass in swirling patterns, or 'spotted' with brightly coloured dots or abstract patterns in red, silver or black.

Complete sets of cocktail glasses are now extremely collectable and, if the shaker is also included, are very desirable. Shakers on their own will start from about £25–£50, and a complete set of glasses and a shaker in plain yellow glass with some banding will be about £100–£150. A very angular Art Deco style set decorated in strong colours can be as much as £300 upwards. Single glasses are considerably cheaper at about £5–£10 each, and it is possible to build up a harlequin set of these for little cost.

Check that there are no chips or cracks – the flared rims on glasses are particularly vulnerable – and check the stem where it meets the bowl, ensuring that it has not been repaired or glued. When buying cocktail shakers, it is important to check that the strainer is included. The glass stopper to the shaker/decanter should be checked for base chips, and also checked to ensure that it matches the shaker and is not a replacement.

coloured glass

Colour has been added to glass since about 1500 BC when it was discovered that adding copper in varying quantities to the mix produced
turquoise, green and red. But it was not until the early 19th century
that coloured glass really came into its own. This was as a result of
experiments in Bohemia (see BOHEMIAN GLASS) when glass such as
Hyalith (yellow) and Lithyalin (predominantly red) was made in
imitation of natural stones. Previously gold had been used to achieve
a ruby red colour and the use of copper was a welcome, cheaper alternative.

In 1851 the Bohemians exhibited their new glassware at the Great
Exhibition in London, and it aroused a great deal of interest with the
British manufacturers. Up until 1845 they had been hampered by
taxation laws, but now the restrictions had been removed and they
were free to experiment with colour and form. In addition, machinery and techniques were vastly improved, and the industry boomed.

Group of late Victorian Cranberry glass items.
LEFT TO RIGHT: clockwise
Cranberry and Vaseline glass sweetmeat dish with frilled edge and clear stem and
foot; £30–£50.
Large jug with enamelled decoration; £60–£100.
Basket with clear glass handle and wide frilled and crimped edge; £60–£80.
Nailsea-style rolling pin with pink and white loops; £30–£60.
Watch stand in clear and cranberry glass with gilt mounts; £80–£100.
Centre: Cranberry sugar shaker with plated top; £25–£35.

ABOVE: Engraved
Bohemian urn and cover
in ruby glass c.1840; £500–£800.
TOP LEFT: Bohemian beaker with
cut red overlay decoration c.1850.
Height 4in, £70–£120.
LEFT: Bohemian lithyalin vase
c.1830; £150–£250.

Various oxides provided varying colours. Pale blue was made by adding copper; reddish blue by adding cobalt; a dark Bristol blue (see BRISTOL GLASS) was achieved by using both cobalt and copper in varying quantities.

Uranium gave a yellow-green and if added in varying quantities, it produced a creamy opalescent shade (see VASELINE GLASS). If antimony was also added, the glass became a topaz colour. Copper oxide could provide a spectrum of colours, ranging from emerald green to blue, light red to pink (see CRANBERRY GLASS). To make a dark red, selenium was added.

Tin or zinc oxide produced 'milk' glass. Previously, 'black' glass had been produced by adding large amounts of manganese or iron oxide to the mix. However, this did not give a true black glass; the manganese showed as deep purple when held up to the light, and the iron oxide as very dark green. Solid black was made by adding iron and/or silver slag.

As the new colours took hold, glass manufacturers began experimenting further. Gradual shading of pale lemon and pink was achieved by Webb (q.v.) with his Queen's Burmese glass (see BURMESE GLASS); Nailsea glass (q.v.) was often striped; Vitro-Porcelain glass (q.v.) was noted for its marbled effect. Aventurine glass was given its glitter by the addition of small flakes of gold or copper to the mix; 'spangled' glass had the addition of flakes of silver or mica. Spatter or end-of-day glass was made by rolling small pieces of variously coloured glass together.

Plain coloured glass was often gilded or enamelled (see MARY GREGORY GLASS). Opaque coloured glass relied on the deep impressed pattern (see PRESS-MOULDED GLASS) for effect. Sometimes the glass was coated with several layers of colours (see CAMEO GLASS), each layer then being cut away in patterns to reveal the one beneath.

When the glass was unornamented in any way, it was blown (see BLOWN AND BLOW-MOULDED GLASS) or pressed (see PRESS-MOULDED GLASS) into attractive shapes. The rims and edges were often waved or crimped, or would be decorated with massive raspberry prunts. Frilled trails or chains of clear glass would swirl decoratively around the piece. The feet on a small bowl, for example,

ABOVE: Detail of raspberry prunt used on Victorian decorative glass.

LEFT: Amethyst spirit bottle c.1840. Height 12in; £350–£450.

Group of late Victorian Vaseline glass items.
LEFT TO RIGHT: clockwise
Vaseline glass beads; £15–£20.
Fluted vase with rustic feet; £30–£50.
Rustic table ornament; £10–£15.
Single epergne with bronzed metal base in the shape of a stag; £50–£75.
Tulip vase on clear welded base; £25–£35.
Rustic table ornament with branched stem; £15–£20.

would be in the shape of small veined leaves. Glass baskets (q.v.) had ornamental handles; small jugs were given added appeal by using threaded glass.

The variety of items produced was enormous: bowls and dishes, cream and sugar sets, jugs, tumblers, decanter sets, centrepieces and épergnes were made for the table. Other items included vases, posy and spill holders, match holders, perfume flasks and bottles, candlesticks, and lampshades, as well as novelties such as bells, pipes, walking sticks, shoes and boots, and rolling pins (see also ÉPERGNES; LAMPSHADES, GLASS; ROLLING PINS; SCENT BOTTLES; SHOES AND BOOTS IN GLASS; and WALKING STICKS).

C

TOP TO BOTTOM: Two Victoria Golden Jubilee plates, 1837–87; Victoria Diamond Jubilee Plate 1837–97; Coronation of George VI plate 1937. Each £15–£20.

· COMMEMORATIVE ·
· PRESSED · GLASS ·

Pressed glass (see PRESS-MOULDED GLASS) was capable of taking a very fine, detailed impression, and this made it an ideal medium for the manufacture of commemorative glass items. Mass-production techniques made it possible for these pieces to be produced in great numbers and many royal commemoratives, especially those of the 20th century, have survived in quantity.

The earliest royal piece is thought to mark the wedding of Queen Victoria's daughter, the Princess Louise, to the Marquise of Lorne (later Duke of Argyll) and a pair of vases was produced in 1872 (a year after their marriage) bearing the couple's portraits, but without inscription. An earlier piece with royal connections had been produced by Greener's (q.v.) in 1870 to celebrate the military successes of Frederick III, the King of Prussia, who had married Victoria's eldest daughter, the Princess Royal, in 1858.

Various glass manufacturers produced souvenirs of both Queen Victoria's Golden (1887) and Diamond Jubilee (1897). The original moulds must have been preserved, for Sowerby's (q.v.) produced an almost identical plate for both events. This has a circular centre panel showing a portrait of the Queen, with the floral emblems of Great Britain in the outer panel.

Designs for royal commemorative pieces were often ornate, showing a portrait, wording, the monarch's crown and, sometimes, the orb and sceptre.

All manner of items were made, ranging from cream jugs and sugar basins to butter dishes, tankards, plates, cups and saucers, and novelties.

Plates were usually made in clear

C

glass, although amber and brown can
also be found. The wording on these
plates consisted of capital letters made
from a number of small raised dots, or
was in smooth glass against a
background that had an orange-peel
texture.

Non-royal commemoratives
celebrated industrial achievements such
as the construction of a high-level bridge
at Newcastle upon Tyne. Famous
figures were immortalised in glass;
statesmen such as Disraeli and
Gladstone, or sportsmen such as the
oarsman Edward Hanlan. The death of
General Gordon was commemorated in
1885, as was the passing of the Jewish
philanthropist Sir Moses Montefiore.
Curiously, no commemorative glass was
issued to mark the death of Prince
Albert, the Prince Consort.

A pressed glass plate was made to
celebrate the Glasgow Exhibition in
1888, and the design is complex, with
the words 'Let Glasgow Flourish' set in
bold letters diagonally across the plate.
The Scottish thistle adorns the outer
panel together with the words 'Glasgow
International Exhibition May 1888'.

Busts of notable figures were
produced and these were in frosted glass
or opaque black. Other figures include
symbolic ones such as Punch and Judy,
John Bull and Britannia.

Prices vary for commemorative glass.
A clear glass plate celebrating the
coronation of George VI in 1937 can be
found for about £10–£15; a Victorian
Golden Jubilee Plate will be about £25–
£35. A sugar bowl (not so collectable) of
the Victorian period will be about £15–
£18. Well-patterned plates marked with
the maker's backstamp are desirable and
will cost about £80 upwards.

As with all press-moulded glass, it is
important to check it carefully before

'Peace and Plenty' jug by
Henry Greener c.1888.
Height 5in; £40–£60.

buying. The complexity of the pattern will often make it difficult to see any damage.

· COMMERCIAL ·
· PERFUME ·
· BOTTLES ·

Up until the turn of the 19th century a woman bought her perfume in a plain bottle from the retailer. It was then taken home and decanted into a superior and more ornate perfume container (see SCENT BOTTLES) that would then stand on the dressing table. However, a Corsican by the name of François Coty changed all that in 1905. He had arrived in France in about 1900 and spent some years studying the perfume industry in Grasse. He launched his first perfume in Paris in 1905 and called it 'La Rose Jacqueminot'.

What attracted women to Coty's perfume, apart from its fragrance, was its packaging – a brilliant stroke of marketing on his part. By 1907, the plain bottle had vanished and in its place was a square bottle of cut glass with a carved stopper. Other perfume manufacturers soon adopted the idea of fancy containers and René Lalique (q.v.), who had been designing the bottles for Coty, was commissioned to make perfume bottles for d'Orsay and Roger et Gallet.

In addition to new shapes and designs for the bottle, Lalique also designed attractive small gold labels. These were intended for the plainer, less decorative bottles.

The new style of bottle dominated the market and they were soon made by companies such as Houbigant, Molinard, Rigaud and so on. Sizes varied from a small handbag vial to large

containers that could be placed on the dressing table. Some were sold in pairs and attractively boxed, or placed in silk-lined caskets.

By the 1920s, the craze for Art Deco (q.v.) swept the country and commercial perfume bottles reflected the trend. Bottles were produced that echoed the geometric shapes and patterns; square bottles were carved or etched with stylised scrolls; triangular bottles would have carved sunray patterns. Stoppers, too, became even more important and often outshone the container.

Fashion designers began bringing out their own brands of perfume. Coco Chanel launched 'Chanel No 5' in 1923. The House of Worth followed suit with its perfume 'Dans La Nuit' the following year. In 1925, Jeanne Lanvin introduced 'My Sin' and at about the same time Elsa Schiaparelli brought out her perfume 'Shocking'. This was packaged in a 'waisted' geometric bottle with flowers adorning the stopper and was contained in a 'signed' navy blue leather case lined with 'shocking' pink satin.

Less extravagant bottles relied on their prettily decorated cardboard

Selection of perfume bottles from the 1930s. On the left is the Bonzo dog bottle. The ball balanced on his nose is the stopper. On the extreme right is a small bottle of 'Evening in Paris' scent.

C

containers for appeal. 'Violettes de Parme' by Giraud Fils of Paris was in a matchbox-type of box which had a label showing the violet. 'Lily of the Valley' perfume was similarly packaged in a cylindrical box.

In the 1930s, novelty bottles appeared. Schiaparelli produced a huge 'sun' which weighed about 3lb (1.3kg). Dubarry bottles were set in a plastic container that had an accompanying pair of dancing figurines. 'Mr Mischief' perfume was sold in a cupid-shaped bottle with a witch's hat, appropriately decorated with stars and crescent moons, as a cover. This type of bottle will cost about £20–£30, whereas a Schiaparelli bottle (with stopper and case) will cost about £60–£80.

Less ornate bottles such as 'Evening in Paris' in its unmistakable dark blue container will be about £15–£20, although they can sometimes be found at flea markets and fairs for far less. A 'Top Hat' bottle and cover will also be about £15–£20. The clear glass 'Bonzo' dog, which was sold by Woolworth's during the 1940s/1950s, will be about £15–£20.

Early Lalique bottles were usually signed, but this signature will often make the price escalate beyond the pocket of the average collector, selling for £500 or £600 upwards depending on size. Bargains can still be found, however – a late Lalique bottle from about 1950, of large size in frosted glass with a gilt stopper, was recently found at an antiques fair for only £20.

Bottles should be examined for chips and cracks. Often there was an inner stopper covered by an outer cap or lid, but one or other of these is often missing, so it is worth checking carefully. Ensure that there is no cracking to any plastic casing.

C

· CRANBERRY · · GLASS ·

This is perhaps the most widely collected glass from the Victorian period, with Vaseline (q.v.) glass a close second, and the familiar raspberry pink shade is often seen at antiques fairs.

Red glass had been produced by the Romans who added copper oxide to their mix. Later, gold chloride was added to produce glass of a rich red. Pale ruby glass, using copper oxide, first appeared in England in the early 19th century but due to the limitations placed on the industry by the tax levy on glass, items in the new glass were mainly of a domestic nature, such as jugs, drinking glasses, custard cups and vases. In 1845, the tax was abolished leaving manufacturers free to experiment with both colour and design.

Manufacture was mainly in the Midlands, Sunderland and Warrington, although the majority was produced in the Stourbridge area. Vast quantities were made and it is impossible to attribute many of the pieces. However, Webb (q.v.) and Richardson (q.v.) can be recognised by their designs, as can Stevens & Williams (q.v.).

A great variety of items were produced. These ranged from decanters and wine glasses to perfume bottles, decorative glass baskets, sweetmeat dishes, cake stands and tazzas, table centrepieces (épergnes), posy holders and vases, match strikers and spill holders, oil lamps and lamp shades, candle holders and lustres and even trinket sets. Novelties were made in the shapes of bells, shoes, rolling pins and walking sticks.

Shapes and decorations became incredibly varied from about 1880. A small cranberry glass vase or jug, for

Basket with deep frilled and crimped rim and clear glass handle, standing on leaf-shaped feet. Height 7in; £60–£80.

Cranberry and Vaseline glass sweetmeat dish with frilled edge and clear glass stem and foot. Height 3½in; £30–£50.

C

Sugar shaker with silver-plated top. Height 5in; £25–£35.

Watch holder with rustic body and clear, reeded glass hook. Height 9in; £50–£75.

example, would have pinched or pincered trails or chains of clear glass winding around it, and it might stand on small feet that were made of leaf shapes in clear glass. The rim or edge might be plain or extravagantly waved, crimped or frilled. Often, 'collars' of clear frilling or 'prunts' were added as extra embellishment.

Cranberry glass was often combined with opalescent or Vaseline glass and the shading of one into the other is most attractive. It was rarely used with any other colour except when cased or overlaid (see CAMEO GLASS) when white was generally employed. The cutting followed the Bohemian style, although not so ornate in style and without the addition of gilding.

Any painting on Cranberry glass was done in enamels and/or sometimes gilt, and this hand-painting was often floral in style, although Mary Gregory (q.v.) glass showed the figures of Victorian children painted in white enamelling.

With the advent of pressed glass (see PRESS-MOULDED GLASS) towards the end of the century and the improvement in mechanisation, the production of Cranberry glass gradually died out and by about 1914 had stopped altogether. Strangely, Cranberry glass was rarely press-moulded but was always hand-blown, although a few of the American glasshouses did produce some pressed examples, but these pieces are rare.

The colour of Cranberry glass resembles warm, runny raspberry jam. For the collector who is just beginning, it is advisable to study Victorian examples in order to recognise this characteristic colour. Cranberry glass is now being reproduced and can sometimes appear at antiques fairs and markets. The modern glass is attractive but tends to have a less warm hue than the older glass and has a slightly bluer tinge to it when held up to the light.

As Cranberry glass is so collectable prices are high. A plain jug of about six inches (15 cm) in height will be about £60–£100; a cake stand about £150–£180, and a small basket with large prunts edging the rim and a clear glass handle will cost about £80–£100. Tiny cream jugs are about £40 upwards while plain glass tumblers cost between £12 and £20.

Where the glass is heavily decorated with trailing chains etc., check carefully for chips, as these are not easily detected. Hold the piece up to the light to check the colour and, if in doubt of its age, do not buy. Reputable dealers will advise if there is any uncertainty.

· CRUETS ·

The word 'cruet' does not just describe salt and pepper sets, but is also used for the ornate sets of many pieces used by the Victorians and Edwardians. The glass containers were generally housed in carrying stands or frames of silver or silver plate and could consist of as many as ten or twelve bottles. Apart from salt,

Cruet set with four cut and hallmarked silver-mounted bottles set in a black papier-mâché frame with brass supports c.1849; £400.

pepper and mustard, cruets stands also held sugar casters, oil and vinegar bottles and various other bottles for different spicy sauces.

The stands varied from simple bases fitted with looped metal holders to contain the bottles to handsome galleried 'trays' with ornate carrying handles. Simple three-piece sets consisted of covered mustard and pepper pots and an open salt, usually square or oval in shape. The pieces were either left plain, or with perhaps a simple ribbed pattern; were press-moulded (q.v.) or could be ornately cut in a strawberry or hobnail pattern (see CUTTING, GLASS).

In larger sets, the sauce, oil and vinegar bottles would resemble miniature decanters (q.v.) with either cut glass stoppers, or plain or pierced caps in silver or plate.

By the end of the 19th century, cruet sets were being made in pottery and porcelain, often to match the china dinner or tea ware, and by the 1920s and 1930s novelty ceramic cruets were being produced providing a cheap alternative to glass.

When buying, it is important to check for chips and cracks in ornately cut cruets and particularly where there are matching glass stoppers. Check also that the stoppers fit tightly; any looseness will indicate a mismatch. Salt often attacks the surface of a glass container making it cloudy in appearance and this

Three-piece cruet in silver-plated stand c.1930; £25–£40.

C

cloudiness cannot be removed. Salt will also corrode metal caps and tops, so check these carefully. If the stand is of silver, check for the hallmarks which will authenticate and date the piece. The letters EPNS stand for electro-plated nickel silver and some early plated items have the addition of various shields and initials which were intended to fool the unwary into thinking the piece was silver, so ensure the hallmarks (q.v.) are genuine. Where the stands are plated, ensure that the plating is still bright and good and not yellowed or worn.

Prices are high for multi-container sets and they will cost about £1500–£2000 in silver. Plated Victorian sets are cheaper and a set with five containers will be about £150–£200. Three-piece sets of salt, pepper and mustard, either plain or in pressed glass, can be found at auction for about £15–£20 upwards, a little more if the glass is attractively wheel cut. (See also SALTS.)

· CUSTARD · · CUPS ·

These attractive glass cups were intended to take thick, sweet concoctions such as custard or syllabub. Their period of manufacture is relatively short, dating from the start of the 19th century to about 1920.

Custard cups generally consist of a bowl, a handle and a footed stem, although the latter is sometimes missing so that the custard cup more resembles a small beer tankard or a teacup in style. It is thought that the handles were applied in one of two ways and this will help with the dating: before 1860 the handles were put on from top to bottom and this procedure was reversed after that date.

C

The cups were usually made of clear glass, although examples have been found in pale colours of ruby, amber, yellow and cranberry (q.v.). The shapes varied between a simple rounded cup, a flared waisted 'sherry glass' type and a severe 'bucket' shape.

When made of clear glass, custard cups relied on etched, engraved or cut patterns for appeal. The patterns ranged between simple fluting cut on the wheel, to highly decorative etched designs, and a stylised fern was favoured by the Victorians. The machine-etched 'Greek Key' design was also popular, as were overlapping circles and scrolled patterns. The 'thumb print' or printy was much used throughout the Victorian era, and this was also found on decanters and wine glasses. In fact, custard cups were often made in patterns that matched the suites of wine glasses and decanters of the day (see DECANTERS and DRINKING GLASSES). Occasionally the custard cups were painted with enamelled colours.

Custard cups are still relatively cheap and late Victorian examples in clear glass can be found for about £5 or £10. Earlier glasses will be about £15–£30 and those of coloured glass or having hand-painted decoration will be about double that price. (See also JELLY GLASSES.)

C

· CUTTING ·
GLASS

The cutting of glass was always done by hand-operated machinery, making it a skilled, lengthy and expensive process. As this cutting needed to work on a good depth of glass, the glass was necessarily thick and heavy, and this weight can help in identifying it so that the collector is not confused by moulded glass or pressed glass (see BLOWN AND BLOW-MOULDED GLASS and PRESS-MOULDED GLASS).

There are various basic styles of cutting all of which are designed to bring out the beauty of the glass itself and to provide refractive angles for the best reflection of light.

The earliest cuts were flutes, shallow stepping and shallow diamonds. Prismatic cutting often decorated the edges of bowls and jugs. In later cuts, the hollow diamond was used as were hexagons and crescent or lunar slices. Stars, usually seen on the base of wine glasses or decanters, for example, were

Vase with diamond and fan cutting c. 1850. Height 6¼in; £50–£70.

C

Small cut glass vase
c.1940; £15–£20.

Cream jug by John Ford of
Edinburgh c.1920; £30–
£50.

shallow with six or twelve 'rays', only later becoming more deeply cut and executed in more complex patterns.

Gradually, the hollow diamond motif became much more open in style and larger in size. Relief diamonds developed into tiny, sharply-pointed diamonds contained within a larger diamond, or set in panels within a cut diamond shape to achieve a chequered effect. These were known as strawberry diamonds. Sometimes tiny relief-cut diamonds covered the entire surface of the piece or were set in panels or gadroons. Hobnail cutting consisted of a star cut into the top of a flat, polished diamond and these star-cut diamonds were often set close together for an all-over effect.

The advent of cheap, mass-produced pressed glass towards the end of the 19th century led to the decline of cut glass. It is therefore of antique age and good pieces can be very expensive to buy.

Cut glass should feel sharp to the touch and once compared with moulded glass can be easily recognised: cut glass is heavier in weight, will sparkle well, and have a good 'ring' if gently tapped or 'pinged' with the fingernail. Moulded glass, on the other hand, is lightweight by comparison, will feel smoother, and will often show the mould lines which have been imperfectly polished out.

When buying cut glass, it is important to check for cracks and large chips. However, smaller chips to the surface on early pieces are often unavoidable and these should make little difference to the collector, apart from price.

Prices will vary between £40–£50 for a small jug with hobnail cutting to £250–£300 for a water jug with prismatic and diamond cutting and a scalloped rim.

d

· **DAVIDSON** ·
GEORGE & CO

The Davidson glassworks was founded in 1867 but, although it became one of the more famous glasshouses in north-east England, the owner, George Davidson, did not enter the field of glassmaking until he was 45 years of age. The son of a miller, and one of twelve children, Davidson was chiefly a jobbing builder, then a butcher. He owned shares in several companies, was a considerable property owner, a councillor, and had a finger in several local pies.

He built his glassworks at Teams in Gateshead and began the successful manufacture of paraffin lamp chimneys with a small team of workers. Despite a serious fire in 1881, the firm continued to expand, moving into the more ornamental field of pressed glass (see PRESS-MOULDED GLASS). By buying up the moulds of several other glass manufacturers, Davidson was able to produce an extremely comprehensive range of patterns and designs and by 1887 the company had a workforce of 350 men and was firmly established as a leading glassworks.

Large-footed sugar bowl pressed in a hobnail pattern c.1885; £20–£30.

In 1895, the company introduced Pearline (q.v.) to the public and the following year saw a translucent glass in a pale ruby colour which was called Patent Rose. In 1910, Davidson's patented their flower block, a solid dome of glass that was pierced with holes to take the stalks of flowers. Perhaps their most famous glass, however, was the streaked Cloud Glass (q.v.) which was introduced in the 1920s.

In the 1930s, Davidson's purchased the moulds of Chippendale glass. This clear glass with its pattern of small inward curving panels had first been manufactured in America in 1907, and was registered by the Jefferson Glass Company in 1911. It proved very popular and, in the 1920s, large amounts were being exported to the National Glass Company in Britain. In 1930, this company acquired the Chippendale moulds and had the glass made at Davidson's factory. However, Davidson's bought the moulds outright in 1933.

Like other makers of pressed glass, Davidson's had their own trademark, although it was never formally registered. It was used for only about ten years, between 1880–90, and took the form of a demi-lion rising from a mural crown (see MAKERS' TRADEMARKS). Chippendale glass is recognisable from its pattern. The American glass bears the name Chippendale Krystol. Glass from the 1920s often bears a registered design number (see REGISTERED DESIGN NUMBERS) and that made by Davidson carried a paper label.

· DECANTERS ·

Up until the 17th century wine and ale had been contained in earthenware bottles. When glass bottles appeared early in that century, they were made of dark green or dark brown glass. In the 1670s, George Ravenscroft perfected the technique of making lead glass and this meant that bottles of clear glass were stronger and less brittle than before. In 1745 glass items were taxed by weight and so decanters which had formerly been of a heavy design now became finer and more delicate.

Gradually the design of the decanter changed and developed. The mallet shape of the mid-18th century gave way to a decanter with a wider base and a

Green tapered spirit decanter with two neck rings and lozenge stopper c.1780. Height (less stopper) 9in; £350–£400.

d

shorter neck and this, in turn, was superseded by a drum shape in the Regency period. Straight-sided decanters with square bases were also introduced around this time, and these held either wines or spirits.

In the Victorian era decanters were often made in sets of two, four or six. These were kept on the sideboard and were often held in a wooden, silver or plated frame known as a tantalus. The frame often had a retaining bar across and this was kept locked, presumably so that the servants could not help themselves to the liquor.

With their love of novelty, the Victorians decided that different drinks should be kept in differently shaped decanters. The 'onion' decanter with its wide globular base and long slender neck, also known as a globe and shaft decanter, frequently held sherry, while claret was contained in a decanter with a metal handle, collar and lid (see CLARET JUGS). Whisky and other spirits were kept in straight-sided decanters that had squared-off corners. Ships' decanters had a wide heavy base for stability on

d

'Onion' sherry decanter in cut glass with cut glass stopper c.1880. Height 10½in; £50–£80.

board a rolling vessel.

Ornamentation on Victorian decanters was varied. Early examples had 'ringed' necks and were delicately engraved with vine leaves and grapes, or they would have panels or pillars cut into the glass. Later 'onion' decanters were often plain relying only on 'thumb print' indentations for decoration. Others were finely engraved or machine etched in a series of scrolled, zigzag or Greek key patterns. Spirit decanters were invariably heavily cut in perhaps a diamond or hobnail pattern, for example (see CUTTING, GLASS).

Miniature decanters are sometimes travellers' samples, but are more likely to be cruet bottles (see CRUETS) which once held oil, vinegar or various sauces.

Very early decanters are costly for the collector to buy; those of the mid-to-late Victorian era are more affordable. An 'onion' sherry decanter will cost about £50–£80, depending on the amount of decoration; a square-bodied whisky decanter with deep cutting will be about £80–£120. An Edwardian decanter with a long narrow neck and fluted rim decorated with a machine engraved pattern will be about £40–£60.

LEFT: Cylindrical decanter with flute and diamond cutting and cut mushroom stopper c.1820. Height (less stopper) 9in; £200–£250.
RIGHT: Ovoid spirit decanter, flute cut, and with hollow mushroom stopper c.1840. Height 7in; £50–£70.

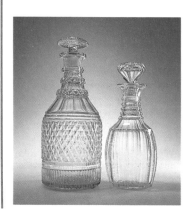

Miniatures cost about £10–£20 upwards.

When buying a decanter, it is important to check that the stopper is original (see DECANTER STOPPERS). It should fit firmly. According to experts, a decanter should be capable of being lifted (when empty) by its stopper, as this was always ground to fit tightly into that particular decanter and no other. However, this is not a practice that is recommended when buying, as accidents can – and do – happen. Stoppers that are loose or wobbly will not be original. Compare the colour of the stopper with that of the decanter, as even clear glass can vary in tone, and check that any cutting matches the design of that on the decanter.

Check for chips on the rim of the decanter and on the stopper, and also examine any cutting on the body for chips. These will not necessarily detract from the usefulness of the decanter and can, in fact, reduce the price to an affordable level but, when buying, the purchaser should be aware of any faults. Tiny rim chips on either decanter or stopper can be ground down, but those that are too large or too deep will devalue the piece.

Avoid any decanters that are badly scratched inside. Some interior stains will respond to the pouring of vinegar inside, after washing with detergent, and letting it stand overnight. The stains should then be gently rubbed with tissue or a soft cloth which has been wrapped around a length of bent wire. Any bloom or heavy clouding will have to be professionally removed. A washed decanter should never be put away wet. Allow it to dry without the stopper; any remaining condensation can be removed by drying the interior with a hairdrier.

'Bristol blue' spirit decanter with ovoid body, decorated with simulated gilt wine label and gilt decoration c.1800. Height 7½in. One of a set of three, comprising Rum, Brandy, and Hollands (Gin); £1000–£1500 for the set.

Barrel-shaped blue spirit decanter with gilt staves and oval 'Rum' label. Gilded ball stopper c.1840. Height 6¼in. One of a set of three, comprising Rum, Whisky, and Brandy. £900–£1100 for the set.

·DECANTER· ·STOPPERS·

These are sought after in their own right and can often form an attractive collection. They will also help in dating the decanter they accompany.

The spire stopper first appeared in about 1770, while the flat target or 'bull's eye' stopper dates back to about 1780 and this can be found either cut or moulded. The lozenge and mushroom shaped stopper made their appearance in about 1800, and the latter was frequently cut in a pattern that matched the decanter. Pear-shaped stoppers were used with ringed neck decanters of about 1810.

Hollow stoppers of about 1850–60 were often star cut on their flattish tops. Others with more rounded tops would be cut in panels or 'thumb prints' to match the decanter. Dome-shaped stoppers could be cut, or the dome could be adapted into a jelly-mould shape.

Square spirit decanters could have large round ball-like stoppers that were heavily faceted, or large flattish stoppers that were ornately cut. 'Onion' decanters had round stoppers that tapered into the ground portion so that

Selection of decanter stoppers; £2–£10 each.

they stood proud of the neck of the decanter.

Stoppers can often be found on their own, and can be bought quite cheaply at flea markets and some antiques fairs. They will be about £2–£5 upwards, while ornate and coloured examples will cost more. Check for chips to the flat interior surface before buying, although small chips can be successfully ground down. Chips to the cut or faceted surfaces will detract from the value.

· DERBYSHIRE ·
JOHN & CO

There can be some confusion about Derbyshire glass as the first glassworks was set up in Hulme, Manchester, in 1858 by a James Derbyshire, and it is not clear what his relationship was to John Derbyshire. The factory was called the British Union Flint Glass Works, and in 1868 another factory was opened – the Bridgewater Flint Glass Works. Two years later, the name of the latter was changed to J., J. and T. Derbyshire (James, John and Thomas). A number of designs were registered under the names of both factories from 1864–6.

In 1873, John Derbyshire set up on his own at Regent Street, Salford, trading as John Derbyshire. The name was changed to John Derbyshire & Co in 1875, and to the Regent Flint Glass Co in 1877. Designs were registered during these four years, but none after that, and it is thought that John might have rejoined the family firm, as designs were still being registered to James Derbyshire & Sons of both Hulme in Manchester and Regent Street in Salford in the early 1880s.

The best known of John Derbyshire's pressed glass (see PRESS-MOULDED GLASS) are the figures and animals

modelled as paperweights and/or
ornaments. The recumbent lion was
taken from Landseer's design for those
at the foot of Nelson's Column, and was
made in clear glass of various colours,
including black, and in frosted glass.
Recumbent dogs, such as greyhounds
and collies, were also made. Figures
were modelled after Punch and Judy,
Britannia, Queen Victoria, and a Greek
winged sphinx was produced in 1876 in
both clear and frosted glass.

John Derbyshire's mark shows the
monogram JD set across an anchor (see
MAKERS' TRADEMARKS), and is often
accompanied by a registered design
lozenge (see REGISTERED DESIGN
NUMBERS).

· DISASTER ·
· GLASS ·

This dates from the 19th century and
production seems confined to the north-
east of England. Glass goblets were
made to mark tragic events and disasters
but not from any ghoulish desire for
profit, rather as an aid to help the
surviving victims.

The glass is usually pressed or blown
(see BLOWN AND BLOW-MOULDED
GLASS, and PRESS-MOULDED GLASS) and
is of cheap quality, and the engraving is
often poorly or badly done. The glass
was inscribed with details of the disaster
that had occurred, and was sold to raise
money for the survivors and the
dependants. Details of the happening
were faithfully recorded – a goblet made
at the time of an explosion at Hetton
Colliery, for example, bears the
inscription: 'Hetton Colliery Explosion,
20 Dec. 1860. 22 lives lost'.

When 191 children were crushed to
death at the Victoria Hall in Sunderland
in 1883, a disaster fund was set up and

the sale of Victoria Hall glasses contributed to this. These glasses were made so swiftly after the tragedy that the inscription erroneously reads: 'Victoria Hall Disaster, 16 June 1883. 182 children lost'. It was only later that nine more children died of their injuries but by then the goblets had already been inscribed.

Disaster glass is not too plentiful and will need searching out. Prices vary between £20–£40 for examples with simple inscriptions; those of more complex pattern or recording famous disasters will cost £100 and over.

· DOMES, GLASS ·
AND THEIR CONTENTS

The Victorians kept all manner of things under tall glass domes. Perhaps the most commonly seen were the stuffed birds found in the gentleman's study or the drawing room. The display usually consisted of several birds artistically mounted on a lichen-covered branch, with a decorative arrangement of dried grasses at the base. The birds were

Large glass dome containing wax fruit on velvet-lined base; £50–£100.

d

invariably small in size, larger examples usually being placed in glass-fronted boxes.

Flower arrangements were also popular and these consisted of dried blooms, artificial silk flowers, or displays made using shells and/or colourful dyed feathers. Clocks appeared under glass domes, as did model ships, and wooden or ceramic figures. Queen Victoria also set the fashion for having her children's hands modelled in unglazed porcelain and set beneath a dome.

The glass dome was intended to protect the contents and was made to fit snugly on to a wooden base. Those enclosing stuffed birds would have been hermetically sealed for preservation. Shapes varied from the tall, column-like dome with its rounded top, to oval-shaped domes of large size.

The domes were extremely fragile and were easily broken. If searching for a replacement dome, it is essential to know the exact measurements of the base, including the indentation or slot that the dome would have fitted into securely. Any slight chipping to the base is acceptable, but cracks should be avoided as these may spread and make the dome worthless.

An antique or Victorian dome will cost from about £30–£50 upwards, depending on its size, and will be more if the original base is present. Reproduction glass and acrylic domes (with or without wooden bases) ranging in height from 1 inch (2.5 cm) to 24 inches (70 cm) (glass) and 2 inches (5 cm) to 10¾ inches (27 cm) (acrylic) can be purchased, and retailers often advertise in antiques or antique clocks magazines. An acrylic dome should never be used to cover a clock as the plastic will adversely affect the clock's movement and workings.

Narrow glass dome on mahogany base, containing shaving from whalebone washed up on Hastings beach c.1880 (Hastings Museum).

· DRINKING ·
· GLASSES ·

Unlike Regency and earlier glasses, 19th-century drinking glasses can be found reasonably cheaply and an attractive collection can be built up without too much outlay.

From about 1830, the previously short stems on wine glasses lengthened and these longer stems were made in simple or baluster shapes, or were ornamented with plain or cut knops. By the middle of the century, the bowls had become less conical or bucket-shaped, and were comfortably rounded or bell-like. This was also the time when the saucer-shaped champagne glass was introduced in place of the tall fluted glass.

Early Victorian glasses were usually cut, the pattern being done by hand on a copper wheel. The glass tended to be thick in order to accommodate a good depth of cutting. Cased glass (see CAMEO GLASS) wine glasses are expensive, and a cheaper alternative are those with stained or flashed bowls. The cutting away of the coloured glass on the

LEFT TO RIGHT: Dwarf ale glass with flammiform wrythen bowl and folded foot c.1740; £220–£280. Dwarf ale glass with wrythen-moulded bowl and plain foot c.1815; £30–£50. Dwarf ale glass with flute-moulded bowl and plain foot c.1810; £30–£50.

d

English champagne glass in Venetian revival style c.1870; £30–£50.

latter was sometimes done in a series of shallow star cuts or more ornately in a pattern of fruiting vine leaves. There was very little depth of cutting involved as the 'layer' of coloured glass was so thin.

In the 1860s, the etching of glass was mechanised. The design was scratched on to the glass which had been previously coated with an acid-resistant substance. When the glass was subsequently dipped in hydrofluoric acid, the pattern was etched into the glass. The Greek key pattern was popular, as were repeat patterns of concentric circles, and closely overlapping curves. Naturalistic designs included flowers that resembled daisies and cornflowers, or vines and grapes.

Pressed glass (see PRESS-MOULDED GLASS) was introduced in the latter half of the 19th century. This made it possible for wine glasses to be made in imitation of cut glass, and these were available to the public at far less cost.

By the end of the century, large suites of glasses were being produced and the 1907 Army & Navy Stores catalogue shows suites consisting of twelve sherries, ports, clarets, champagnes, and six liqueurs. Also included were twelve tumblers (q.v.), twelve finger glasses (finger bowls), two

Two from a set of blue flashed sherry glasses with diamond and fan cutting c.1880. £60–£80 for a set of six.

86

d

Etched wine glasses in two sizes with diamond and scroll design c.1930; £8–£15 each.

caraffes [sic] with tumblers, two quart decanters (q.v.), and a claret jug (q.v.). The complete suite added up to 85 pieces. Soda tumblers, ice plates, jelly glasses (q.v.), custard glasses (see CUSTARD CUPS) and pint decanters were available as matching optional extras.

When buying drinking glasses, check for rim chips, and ensure that the rim and/or foot has not been ground down to eliminate previous damage. As a rough guide, the diameter of the foot should equal that of the bowl, or be slightly larger, but never smaller.

Heavily cut glasses will be about £40–£50 each, but good quality pressed glass examples can be found for about £5–£15. A maker's mark (see MAKERS' TRADEMARKS) can sometimes be found on the glass. This was often placed inside the glass where the bowl met the foot. It can often be detected by touch rather than by seeing it on the clear glass.

Acid etched glasses can still be found quite cheaply. A set of six tumblers with an attractive floral design was recently purchased for only £5 from a junk shop. Single, stemmed wine glasses with a Greek key or concentric circle pattern will be about £2–£5 depending on size. Flashed glass liqueur glasses will be about £5–£8 each, but a set of six will cost about £60–£80.

One of a set of four green wine glasses with flute-cut conical bowls and facet-cut knopped stems on plain feet c.1840; £300–£400 the set.

e

· EPERGNES ·
VICTORIAN

These ornate table centrepieces which were intended to hold flowers or sweetmeats, or simply to be decorative, were much loved by the Victorians. By the turn of the century they had lapsed into disuse and a copy of 'Mrs Beeton's Everyday Cookery and Housekeeping Book' dating from 1904 admonishes the young housewife that 'this is not the age for heavy dinners nor heavy decorations. Substantial entrées, immense joints, and old ports have departed with the solid masses of flowers filling the massive épergnes'.

The épergne referred to in the book was extremely ornate. Standing as much as 30 inches (76 cm) high, it consisted of a frilled glass dish (or sometimes a flat mirrored base). In the centre, an arrangement of brass collars held a central upright trumpet of glass, while two or three other trumpets flared out symmetrically. Sometimes, twisted canes of glass accompanied the trumpets, and these would end in a scrolled curve from which was suspended a small glass basket. The épergnes were made in pink (see CRANBERRY GLASS), opalescent yellow (see VASELINE GLASS), or opalescent glass combined with cranberry, pale turquoise or green. The coloured trumpets were left plain or had pinched or frilled trails of glass winding around them. The flared opening was also sometimes frilled and pinched.

Single épergnes of trumpet shape could be made, standing on a footed stem, or the conical base could be held in a silver, silver plated, or base metal holder. The holders were often simple in design, being additionally decorated with applied metal leaves. Small cast

Vaseline glass épergne set in a dished base, and having one large and three smaller trumpets edged with green and decorated with trails of clear green glass. Late Victorian. Height 21in; £250–£300.

animals such as deer sometimes stood on a base resembling a grassy mound.

Many-branched metal holders can also be found and these support small, clear glass posy vases in a horizontal arrangement of varying height.

Large, ornate épergnes will cost between £250–£400 so, if buying one of these, it is important to check very carefully for any damage to the pinched trails of glass. Chips can easily be missed in the profusion of frills. The trumpets were supported in their brass collars by a plaster of Paris mixture and if this is not sound, it will make the arrangement of trumpets very insecure. The plaster can be renewed, but only by an expert.

Single épergnes in glass will cost from about £15 upwards for a clear example to about £50–£75 or more for one in Vaseline glass. Clear glass épergnes in plain plated holders can be found at auctions for about £15–£20; coloured or opalescent glass in decorative holders will be about £70 upwards, depending on size and design. When buying single épergnes in holders, ensure that the glass is a snug fit. It should feel firm and secure, and should not wobble.

Single trumpets from a larger épergne set are also collectable, and can make an attractive display. These can be found for about £20 upwards each, depending on size and colour.

Pair of metal mounted single épergnes, the base in the shape of a stag. £50–£75 each; £120–£170 the pair.

· EYE · BATHS ·

Although silver, porcelain and earthenware eye baths had been used in Britain since the beginning of the 17th century, they were not made in glass until the late 1670s. Initially, the glass baths followed the style of those made in other materials and consisted of a large bowl set on a footed base. This

e

pedestal shape was continued, with modifications, into the 20th century.

The two other shapes that came later are the reservoir or 'fish bowl' eye bath that was made in pressed glass (see PRESS-MOULDED GLASS), and this has a double-gourd-like body. The other design was the unstemmed 'bucket' shape that is still being made today.

Coloured glass, as well as clear, was used for eye baths from about 1780, and they were made in dark 'Bristol' blue (see BRISTOL GLASS), dark green, and, more rarely, in amethyst. Later colours are purple (rare), yellow, amber, brown, green, blue, and turquoise (rare).

Early 20th-century eye baths sometimes carry a patent and/or trademark (see MAKERS' TRADEMARKS) on the base which can help with dating and identification.

Prices vary considerably, and range between about £5 for a press-moulded pedestal eye bath in clear glass, to £10–£12 for a similar example in coloured glass. Rare colours such as turquoise will be about £30–£50 depending on design, while amethyst can command double or treble that amount.

The dark blue liners intended for silver and plated salts and cruets are sometimes mistaken for unstemmed eye baths, but if it feels comfortable and makes a good seal in the eye socket, then it is the real thing.

Selection of pedestal and bucket-shaped eye baths in clear glass, green and blue; £5–£12.

· FAIRY · LAMPS ·

The name of Samuel Clarke is always connected with these pretty glass nightlight holders. In fact, Clarke manufactured only the wax nightlights, having the glass holders and shades made by several glass companies, both in England and on the Continent.

Samuel Clarke took out his first patent in the 1880s, and the polite world was astonished when the attractive 'fairy lamps' made their appearance on the dining table. Up until then, nightlights had been used only the sickroom or a child's bedroom. Clarke received further publicity when he donated several thousand of his lamps for use at the fêtes given by the Royal Botanical Society.

The glass holders were first made by Stuart & Sons of Stourbridge, but were often stamped with Clarke's name, 'Clarke's Patent Trade Mark Fairy' or 'S. Clarke Fairy Pyramid'. The word 'Pyramid' referred to the squat candle which was intended to burn for anything between four and eleven hours. Additionally, the glass holders would be stamped with the logo of a fairy holding a wand in her hand (see MAKERS' TRADEMARKS).

The lamps consisted of a dish base into which was placed the nightlight. The cover was dome-shaped and had a central hole for the release of the heated air. The base could be plain, giving the united pieces the look of an egg in its cup, or could be attractively frilled. It was recommended that the nightlight should stand in about a quarter of an inch of water for safety and a decorative advantage was taken of this precaution when flowers and leaves were tucked into the base, encircling the lamp in a pretty floral arrangement. The lamps were made in colours of pink, yellow, and blue, in clear or opal glass, and could be striped or given an acid etched 'satin' finish. They could also have a threaded glass decoration or have crinkled tops.

Webb (q.v.) made fairy lamps in their famous Burmese Glass (q.v.). This attractive yellow/pink glass was either left plain, or could be decorated with a pattern of flowers, fruit and/or leaves.

In 1889, Samuel Clarke registered the trade name 'Cricklight'. This referred to a clear glass shade that stood on a high column-like base. The style had been produced earlier in Burmese glass but was then marketed under the name of 'Fairy'. The Cricklight cast a greater light over a wider area and gradually became more popular than the Fairy Lamp, although these were still being made in 1907. Some Cricklights were made in imitation of the branched candelabra and could have anything from two to four or more shades. The bases were made in pressed glass (see PRESS-MOULDED GLASS), cut glass (see CUTTING, GLASS), porcelain, or silver plate.

Fairy lamps are not easy to find and it is best to seek out a specialist dealer. A good example in machine-pressed glass will cost about £50–£75; a fairy lamp in undecorated Burmese glass by Thomas Webb will cost as much as £300–£400.

· FAIRY · LIGHTS ·

The earliest glass fairy lights appeared in about 1890, and these are the easiest to find and cheapest to buy today. They consisted of small glass 'jars' about three to four inches (8 to 10 cm) in height, moulded into a honeycomb pattern (see BLOWN AND BLOW-MOULDED GLASS and PRESS-MOULDED GLASS). They were fitted with wire handles for hanging, although these handles are nearly always missing nowadays. A small candle or nightlight would be put in the holder which would then be hung on the Christmas tree, or stand on a shelf in the drawing room. At other times, the fairy lights would illuminate a conservatory or be placed among the branches of trees in the garden.

Colours were usually green, brown, amber and a dull blue. Ruby, blue, jade, turquoise, lemon and amethyst are more rare, as are any in opalescent glass (see VASELINE GLASS).

The first electric fairy lights made their appearance at the turn of the century, and were largely imported. Fruits, flowers and lantern shapes made in opaque glass were hand painted, and plain globes were decorated with flowers and/or leaves. Occasionally, they had long silk tassels.

The best hunting ground for these sets of lights are jumble sales, flea markets and auctions. Boxed sets are desirable, but the cardboard container is often torn or shabby. Check that the hand-painted design is not too worn or flaked. Some of these lights still work but replacement bulbs are a problem. Never use them without having the wiring checked by a professional, as old wiring can be dangerous and can lead to fires. An unboxed set will cost about £15–£30; a shabby boxed set will be about £25–£50; and a mint set can be over £100. All these prices, however, depend on the condition of the lights and how elaborate their design.

The glass fairy lights of jar-shape are still relatively cheap and can be found for £3–£8 each. The rarer colours will be about £8–£15; those in opalescent glass £25–£30 upwards.

Clear and brown glass fairy lights; £3–£8.

f

·FLASHED·
·GLASS·
See Cameo Glass

·FRIGGERS·

The word 'frigger' is a traditional and colloquial term used for a variety of novelties made by the glassworkers. They were produced to demonstrate the glassmaker's skill and were generally made after hours using the pieces of left-over glass known as end-of-day glass. Apprentices also made friggers, but these pieces have a more clumsy appearance, as they were intended to test and increase their skill in glassmaking.

A variety of items were produced, such as bowler and top hats, walking sticks and shepherds' crooks, tobacco pipes, rolling pins, bells, and glass 'dumps' (see PAPERWEIGHTS) that were used as door stops or paperweights depending on how large they were.

Glass hats will cost about £60–£160 each; a tobacco pipe about £80–£100; and a green glass 'dump' will be about £40–£50 upwards depending on size. (See also BELLS; ROLLING PINS; WALKING STICKS.)

LEFT TO RIGHT: Nailsea hat in clear glass with opaque white looping c.1850. Height 2½in; £120–£160.
Nailsea hat in pale green crown window glass c.1800. Height 4in; £120–£160.
Nailsea hat in olive green glass with white marvered inclusions c.1810. Height 3¼in; £120–£160.
Note: Later Victorian hats are £60–£100.

LOWER LEFT: Pair of Nailsea-style knitting needles c.1860. Length 12in; £15–£20 the pair.
RIGHT: Nailsea-style pestle c.1860. Length 23in; £80–£100.

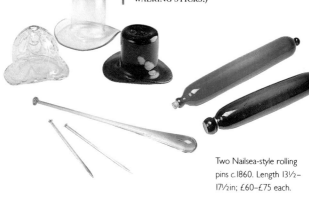

Two Nailsea-style rolling pins c.1860. Length 13½–17½in; £60–£75 each.

· GALLÉ ·
EMILE

Born in 1846, in Nancy, France, Emile
Gallé was the son of a prosperous
manufacturer and designer of pottery
who also had an interest in glassware.
His father ensured Emile's education
and had him trained in both pottery and
glassmaking. In 1874, Gallé took over
his father's business and built it into one
of the largest and most successful
factories in Europe. He was also to have
a profound influence over the other
designers and craftsmen of the day with
his super band innovative creations.

Gallé is best known for his carved
and etched glass (see CAMEO GLASS) on
which the designs appeared to be
sculpted into the metal in high relief.
The best pieces were produced by
wheel cutting through two or three
layers of glass; other examples were acid
etched and then finished off by wheel
cutting. Lesser pieces were acid etched
only. Designs were of a naturalistic
form, reflecting Gallé's love of nature
and his studies as a botanist.
Dragonflies, beetles and butterflies were
set next to realistic blossoms of irises
and lilies, and leaves and flowers swirled
artistically in Art Nouveau fashion on
vases. Colours were rich and vivid.

The cameo glass was introduced in
about 1889, and was an immediate
sensation, but Gallé had already made a
name for himself with his designs in
clear enamelled glass. These showed
Venetian and Islamic influences and
Gallé exhibited them at the Paris
Exposition in 1878. 'Clair de Lune'
followed, which was a transparent glass
with a hint of blue and a touch of
opalescence. He also experimented with
metallic oxides, producing glass that
resembled natural stones such as agate

Vase with enamel and gilt
decoration in design of
thistles and a beetle.
Known as 'verreries
parlantes' (speaking
glassware) because of the
quotation engraved into
the base from which Gallé
had obtained his
inspiration for the piece
c.1880. Height 11½in;
£1000+.

Small cameo flower vase overlaid with dark brown floral decoration c.1900. Signed Gallé. Height 3½in; £1000+.

A large Gray-Stan vase in heavy green glass; £100–£200.

or jade.

In 1897, he brought out a new glass, 'marquetrie-de-verre', a type of applied glass. This involved pressing semi-molten glass into the surface of the blank while it was still malleable. The decoration was then finished off by hand before the glass cooled too quickly.

Gallé was one of the first to sign his work (see MAKERS' TRADEMARKS), apart from the makers of pressed glass. The signature placed on wheel-cut cameo glass was generally finely engraved, while that on an item that had been acid-etched and wheel-finished was cut in cameo and extremely stylised, more of a hieroglyphic in fact. Acid-etched pieces also bore a cameo signature, but of a simplified version. After Gallé's death, signatures were preceded by a star.

· GRAY-STAN · · GLASS ·

The studio producing this glass was established by Mrs Elizabeth Graydon-Stannus in 1926, although she had previously set up a glassmaking studio making reproduction Irish glass in about 1922. However, the new studio concentrated on the making of original coloured glass having pastel and shaded effects.

She started with a small team of about a dozen workers and even at the height of her success, did not employ more than thirty. The factory produced handmade pieces of style and originality, and great emphasis was placed on inventiveness and experimentation with ideas and techniques.

Clear glass would be coated with one or more layers of white or coloured enamel powder while still molten, being dipped into clear glass again before being blown. The initial layer of enamel was often white and this gave the finished glass a colour peculiar to the Gray-Stan studio.

The glass could also be pulled or combed in the Nailsea style (see NAILSEA GLASS and NAILSEA-STYLE GLASS), trailed in spiral, festoon or abstract patterns. It could also be attractively clouded or marbled within a clear glass casing. Some was hand engraved, the nude female form being deeply engraved into clear glass, for example.

Production ceased in 1936, and although some glass was unmarked, most of it bears the name Gray-Stan, both with and without the hyphen.

Gray-Stan vase in mottled green glass. Height 6in; £150–£200.

· **GREENER** ·
HENRY & CO (1820–82)

The son of a glass engraver, Henry Greener began his life in glassmaking when, at the age of 12, he was apprenticed to a glass manufacturer in Gateshead, later working for Sowerby (q.v.). He became a partner in the Sunderland firm of The Wear Flint Glassworks in 1858 and took over sole ownership in 1869.

Despite financial problems in the late 1870s, Greener began to expand his range from domestic items of tableware to novelty pieces in pressed glass (see PRESS-MOULDED GLASS). He manufactured the new Vitro-Porcelain (q.v.), copied from Sowerby and Davidson (q.v.), and imitated the new marbled and malachite glassware. He also produced lion paperweights reminiscent of Derbyshire's (q.v.).

Some of the factory's finest pieces are the commemorative items Greener had previously produced in partnership with James Angus. Items such as plates,

g

cream jugs, sugar bowls, tankards, and cups and saucers, were made in both clear and opal glass. These marked a diversity of people and occasions, such as the statesmen Gladstone and Disraeli, events commemorating the death of the philanthropist George Peabody in 1869, the State visit of the Princess Royal and her husband to Canada in 1878, and the erection of the Eiffel Tower in 1889.

In 1879, Greener produced a range of 'Roman Tiles' or 'Glass Mosaics'. These were to be used for 'general, ecclesiastical and domestic decoration . . . for window flower boxes, conservatories, sanatoriums and fireplaces, hearths and dados'. The tiles were made in opaque malachite colours of white with blue, green or purple, or in plain colours, including black.

After Henry's death, the company was run by his three executors, but again ran into financial difficulties, and in 1886 was taken over by Jobling (see JOBLING, JAMES A. & CO) who retained the Greener name.

There are two trademarks for Greener (see MAKERS' TRADEMARKS). The first is a demi-lion rampant facing left, holding a five-pointed star in its right paw. This dates from 1875–85. The second mark dating from 1885– 1900 shows a similar lion, this time without the star, and holding a battleaxe between both paws.

A pressed glass plate commemorating the death of the American philanthropist George Peabody (1795–1869); £25–£50.

h

· HALLMARKS ·

Gold and silver have been assayed and marked since the 14th century, and by 1478 a system of complete hallmarking had been devised. This included the assay mark, the town mark, and a date letter, with the occasional addition of the maker's mark. These hallmarks generally run in twenty-year cycles, with the style of the date letter and/or the shield enclosing it being changed at the start of each cycle. For example, a date letter in Gothic script might be followed in the next period by a date letter in italic script.

Among the many assay offices were those in London (a leopard's head), Birmingham (an anchor), Sheffield (a crown), Chester (a shield bearing the Arms of the city), Exeter (a three-towered castle) and Edinburgh (a castle).

The standard for gold is indicated by carat marks, each carat being a twenty-fourth part. This gives a guide to the purity of the gold; an alloy having 22 parts of gold to 24 parts of the whole is classified as 22 carat gold. Pure gold is never used as it is too soft. The standard mark is sometimes shown as 916 (22 carat), 750 (18 carat), 585 (14 carat) and 375 (9 carat). Imported gold carries the same standard marks as those for British gold.

Silver consisting of 958 parts per thousand is known as Britannia silver, and if it consists of 925 parts per thousand, it is called Sterling silver. Import marks are of the same standard.

A turquoise blue hyacinth vase with bulbous body and high collared neck c.1850; £45–£65.

· HYACINTH · · VASES ·

Hyacinths have been popularly grown indoors since the 17th and 18th

99

Four hyacinth vases. Those in clear glass £15–£30 each; the dark blue glass example £40–£70.

centuries in what were then known as 'root glasses'. The hyacinth was deemed to have medicinal properties when the dried roots were ground and used as a diuretic.

The principle of growing hyacinths in a vase or glass was simple. The vase would be filled with water and the bulb placed (root side down) in the 'collar' at the top of the vase. As the bulb began to put out its roots, they would stretch to reach the water below. No soil or earth was needed, the plant obtaining sufficient nutrients from the liquid.

Victorian vases could vary in shape from a tall tapering column of about nine inches (23 cm) in height with a deep collar, to a short-necked, onion shape with a wide frilled collar. Some were of a double-gourd shape. They were made in clear and coloured glass, with blue, green, amber and amethyst or purple being the most popular colours. They were also made in Burmese, Cranberry and Vaseline glass (see BURMESE GLASS, CRANBERRY GLASS and VASELINE GLASS).

Prices start at about £15–£20 for plain glass vases in green or dark blue; turquoise and amethyst examples are about £45–£65; Cranberry and Vaseline glasses will be about £50–£60 each, but if hand-painted and decorated, this price will be doubled.

· INK ·
· BOTTLES ·

With the advent of the penny post, there was an increase in letter writing and a greater demand for ink. It had previously been supplied in earthenware bottles, but glass was proving to be a cheaper medium and glassworks were capable of producing huge batches that consisted of about one million moulded bottles.

These mass-produced bottles were made in light and dark green, various blues, amethyst and amber. Rare colours were amber, cobalt and dark green. Shapes varied from round, squat bottles to square or rectangular shapes, triangular (rare) and octagonal. Novelty shapes were also made, such as cottages, igloos, barrels and umbrellas.

Early blow-moulded inkwells (see BLOWN AND BLOW-MOULDED GLASS) were fitted with a cork rather than a cap or stopper and had a sheared lip.

The bottles were often stamped with the name of the manufacturer of the ink, rather than that of the glass works, for example H. C. Stephens.

The unspillable bottle made its appearance in the late 19th century. The opening was surrounded by hollow glass 'shoulders' and if the pot was tilted

Selection of various ink bottles; £1–£5.

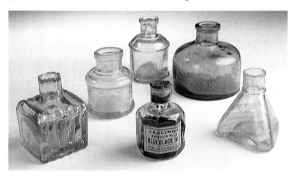

i

the ink flowed into these shoulders rather than spilling out of the central hole. This ink bottle was intended for use in offices, banks and hotels. Later examples had a hole in the base for ease of cleaning, and this was sealed by a rubber stopper or metal screw.

Glass ink bottles are still relatively cheap. The unspillable bottle will cost about £10–£12; sheared lip bottles in pale green glass are about £8–£15; but novelty ink bottles, such as the cottage for example, are very collectable and can cost £80–£100 or more.

Pair of octagonal bottles in pale green glass. Height 2½in; £1–£2 each.

· INKWELLS · & · · INKSTANDS ·

The earliest English inkstands or 'standishes' date from the 17th century, when they were made in silver. Then they consisted of a tray with an inkwell, a container for the wafers, and a sand pot for sprinkling the letter with a powder that absorbed the moisture before being shaken off the paper.

When the fountain pen was invented in the late 1880s, the single inkwell made its appearance. Glass examples can be found with silver, silver-plated, glass, brass and copper lids, all of which are attached by a hinge to a collar of metal around the inkwell. They were made in round or square shapes in cut (see CUTTING, GLASS), pressed or moulded clear glass (BLOWN AND BLOW-MOULDED GLASS and PRESS-MOULDED GLASS).

Nailsea inkwell in pale green crown glass c.1830. Height 2½in; £60–£80.

Victorian souvenir inkwells had a small circular plaque which held a sepia photograph – perhaps of a holiday resort. Tiny inkwells were fixed to the boat-shaped stand, one each side of the central plaque.

Art Nouveau examples (see ART NOUVEAU GLASS) were made in pink

glass (see CRANBERRY GLASS) and enclosed in artistically swirling 'cages' of copper or brass. The matching lid could be plain, or decorated in a relief pattern of flowers or leaves.

Practical inkstands were also made in pressed glass and these usually consisted of a simple glass tray with two matching lidded ink pots.

Single inkwells that were once part of a writing slope can be found quite cheaply. These are always square, usually fairly small, and have metal caps which fit on firmly.

Travelling inkwells consisted of a glass inner enclosed in a leather-covered box of either square or round shape. The hinged top was lined with leather or card and was operated by a spring mechanism which gave a tight seal.

When buying inkwells with glass tops, check that these are well fitting and that they are not replacements. Check also for inner chips; inkwells were used frequently, and sometimes received rough treatment. Check the corners of the inkwells for damage.

Prices will vary from about £8–£15 for a simple example in moulded glass with a flat glass lid; a travelling inkwell in a leather case will be about £15–£20 upwards, depending on size; and an Art Nouveau inkwell in cranberry and copper will be about £60–£80.

Three Victorian lidded inkwells in clear glass; £8–£15 each.

j

· JACOBITE ·
· GLASSES ·

These date from the time of the Jacobite rebellion in the 18th century and are not readily available to the collector. They receive their other name of Amen glasses from the practice of engraving the bowl with a verse or verses taken from the Jacobite anthem. Latin was widely used in Scotland at the time, and Latin tags such as 'Reddas Incolumen' (Restore unharmed) or 'Fiat' (May it happen) are sometimes engraved on to the glass. There is often a cypher JR, or a reference to 'Bonnie Prince Charlie', with sometimes a portrait of the young prince. Patterns could include one of the favourite emblems, such as a star thistle, an oak leaf, a rose, or a bird.

Many reproduction glasses were made in the 19th century and even up until 1930. Early 18th-century glasses of plain design were often later engraved in an effort to deceive.

· JELLY ·
· GLASSES ·

These were usually used for savoury jellies made from ingredients such as calves' feet, although towards the end of the 19th century, gelatine and isinglass were being recommended in cookery books such as Mrs Beeton's 'All About Cookery'. The jelly glasses, however, could also be used for sweet jellies and syllabubs and seem to have been interchangeable with the smaller custard cups (q.v.).

Jelly glasses are of a bell-like or conical shape. The bowl was usually supported by a short stem, although there was sometimes no division

Pair of trumpet bowl jelly glasses with wrythen moulded and notched cut decoration on plain feet c.1780. Height 4in; £80–£90 the pair.

LEFT TO RIGHT: Jelly glass
with bell bowl *c.*1800.
Height 3½in; £30–£45.
Syllabub glass with pan top
bowl *c.*1750. Height 4in;
£80–£100.
Jelly glass with wrythen
trumpet bowl *c.*1800.
Height 4in; £30–£50.

between the bowl and foot. The stem
was always short, but could be knopped.
The bowl was either left plain, was
ribbed or fluted, or could be cut in
facets. The flared rim varied in size, and
was sometimes wider than the foot,
sometimes smaller, or sometimes the
same.

When buying, check for chips and
cracks. Check also that the foot has not
been ground down to cover any damage.
Prices can be low if buying at an auction
or flea market, and a plain jelly glass will
cost about £3–£5. A ribbed or fluted
example will be dearer at about £15–
£20, and one with a heavy knopped
stem and faceted bowl dating from
around 1800 will be about £30–60.

· JOBLING ·
JAMES A. & CO

Although better known for the
decorative pressed glass (see PRESS-
MOULDED GLASS) produced in the
1930s, James Augustus Jobling first
started in business dealing in minerals
and glassmaking chemicals under the
name of Tyne Oil & Grease Works,
supplying among others the firm of
Greener's (q.v.).

j

In 1885, when Greener's faced bankruptcy, Jobling, as one of the firm's principal creditors, took over the company, entering the field of glassmaking for the first time. The name Greener & Co and their trading name of Wear Flint Glass Works were retained until 1921, when it was changed to James A. Jobling & Co, and in 1928 the name was again changed to that of the Wear Glass Works.

In 1921, the company acquired the rights to manufacture Pyrex products from the Corning Glass Works in America. This heat-resistant glass was used for a variety of domestic and laboratory items and was an instant success, proving extremely lucrative.

In the 1930s, the flint glass department of the factory ventured into the production of pressed decorative or 'Art' glass and the Jobling chemists were given the task of developing new types of coloured glass. Such shades as Opalique (an opalescent glass with a blueish tinge), Jade (an opaque green glass resembling the semi-precious stone), Pearl (an opaque glass with a pearly opalescence) and Tortoiseshell (a black and amber glass mix resembling Cloud Glass, q.v.).

The designs on the new glass were executed in relief, and were used on bowls and dishes, water sets, vases and flower blocks, trinket sets and candlesticks, cigarette boxes and ashtrays. The matt or satin finish was achieved by acid-etching.

Celery vases (q.v.) were made which showed realistic bunches of the vegetable in relief on the green glass, although they were also manufactured in the improbable colours of pink, blue and amber, as well as Opalique, now rarely found in a celery vase. The animal world was also featured. Fish and

Pink frosted shallow bowl in 'Fir Cone' pattern, 1934. Registered design number 777133; £15–£30.

bird motifs were used on satin finish vases and table lamp bases, bears on book-ends, and bees on honey-pots.

Flower blocks and bowls often had a female figure as a centrepiece, either a demure Victorian lady, a dancing girl or, more popularly, a scantily draped nude.

Opalique glass was also acid-etched and was used for the manufacture of bowls, dishes and vases, as well as small novelty statuettes such as fish, sea-horses, seals, bears, elephants and other animals, various birds, and butterflies. Opalique was manufactured in imitation of the opalescent glass produced by Lalique (q.v.) in France, and some of the more creative clay models used for the moulds were made by Etienne Franckhauser who also worked for Lalique.

Much of Jobling glass is unmarked other than bearing the catalogue number or the registered design number (q.v.), and because of this, prices can be comparatively low. A green celery vase, for example, will cost from about £15–£25; a flower bowl and block showing a nude will be about £25–£45. Opalescent pieces, however, are more collectable and a small unmarked fish will be about £20–£30. A fruit bowl with flower or pine cone design and registration number will be about £40–£60, but one with a Lalique-style pattern of birds will be more.

Opalescent fruit bowl in 'Flower' pattern, 1934. Registered design number 777134; £40–£60.

k

Pair of faceted knife rests
with 'dumb bell' supports;
£10–£15 the pair.

· KNIFE · RESTS ·

Made in pairs or fours, knife rests were
popular in the late 18th century and
throughout the 19th century, and were
placed on the dinner table to
accommodate the carving knife and fork
when the head of the household was
carving.

Knife rests are usually about four to
five inches (10 to 13 cm) in length.
Some resemble miniature dumb-bells
with their round or octagonal ends cut
attractively in facets. The central bar
was also cut, sometimes more heavily.
Rod or barrel-shaped rests could be
centrally knopped, and cut in a variety
of styles.

Although the majority were in clear
glass, relying on the intricate cutting for
decoration, some coloured examples can
be found. Millefiori glass (see
PAPERWEIGHTS) was also used in various
patterns and some of the Stourbridge
glasshouses would incorporate twists of
threaded glass in red, white and blue in
a latticinio pattern.

Knife rests need careful checking
when buying. Because of the heavy
usage they received there are often tiny
chips to the supporting ends, especially
if these are heavily cut. Ensure also that
the rests are a matching pair.

Bargains can be found at auction,
however, and a pair of plain-cut, faceted
rests can cost as little as £8 or £10. More
ornate examples found at antiques fairs
will be about £10–£20, depending on
the amount of cutting.

One of a pair of knife
rests with carved thistle
design; £15–£20 the pair.

·LACE-MAKERS'· ·LAMPS·

Despite their name, these lamps gave no light on their own. The definition of a lace-maker's lamp is a small table, usually of tripod style, on to which was placed a central candle. The candle was then surrounded by four stemmed glass flasks about five to six inches (12 to 15 cm) high. These flasks were filled with a mixture of distilled spirit and water. The candlelight was then reflected fourfold through the lamps, giving the worker additional light. The lamps also gave a certain magnification, making it easier for the lace-makers to see their work.

The lamps were widely used in the 18th and 19th centuries, and consisted of a candlestick-type base into which was set a globular flask with an open top and a narrow neck, rather resembling an upside-down water carafe. The candlestick base sometimes widened out in the shape of a bell, or could be dished rather like a chamberstick, when the stem would have the addition of a handle for ease of carrying.

A set of four lamps will cost about £150–£180 or more; single examples will vary between about £40–£60. Eighteenth-century lamps start at about £150–£200.

Lace maker's lamp with a double ogee body, drip pan, and a folded conical foot c.1750. Height 5½in; £200–£250.

·LALIQUE·
RENÉ (1860–1945)

Lalique is world famous as a glass designer of great breadth and vision who was foremost in his field. He began by studying drawing and at 16 was apprenticed to a goldsmith. After further studies in Paris and then England he returned to Paris to design jewellery. Much of his inspiration came from

Dragonfly car mascot in clear and etched glass c.1930. Height 8in; £2500+.

Blow-moulded vase with a design of leaping fish c.1920. Height 3in; £700–£1000+.

nature and he used plant, insect and animal forms imaginatively in Art Nouveau style.

Although he had experimented with glass in his workshop, especially with its use in jewellery, and had produced some small glass vessels, it was not until 1905, when he was commissioned to design perfume bottles for François Coty (see COMMERCIAL PERFUME BOTTLES) that Lalique's career in glass design began in earnest. In 1908 Lalique set up his own glass factory at Combs. Ten years later, he opened a new and larger factory at Wingen-sur-Moder in the Rhine district.

Lalique scorned the use of colour in his early glass, although he did use it on rare occasions, and hinted at it in his slightly stained opalescent glass. Instead, he utilised the colourless 'demi-crystal' which had a non-transparent surface. The frosty white of Lalique's glass was compared by his contemporaries to 'the frozen breath of a Polar night', and 'the ethereal brilliance of Arctic ice'.

His career spanned both the Art Nouveau (q.v.) and Art Deco (q.v.) periods, although it is perhaps for his Art Deco work that he is better known. His sculptures of the nude male and female form were often made in opalescent glass and were sometimes set on a bronze base that concealed a light.

Lalique turned to nature for many of his ideas and used fish, animals, birds, flowers, leaves and fruit extensively on bowls, vases and lampshades. One of his best-known designs is 'coquilles' which shows a pattern of shells.

His car mascots were first seen in the 1920s. Perhaps the most famous is that of a girl with streaming hair called 'Victoire' or 'Spirit of the Wind'. Lalique used the naked form again in the 'Archer' which shows a kneeling man holding a bow and arrow within a clear disc of glass. In 1925, when he was commissioned by the car manufacturers, Citroën, to design a new mascot for their latest model, the '5 cheveaux', he produced a mascot appropriately showing five leaping horses. Other designs feature birds such as the falcon, a diving swallow, a crouching guinea fowl and a cockerel, fish such as the perch, and insects like the dragonfly.

Lalique's work was almost always signed (see MAKERS' TRADEMARKS). The signature, R. Lalique, was etched in script or acid-etched, sand-blasted or moulded in block letters. After his death his son Marc carried on the business as 'Cristal Lalique' and pieces were signed simply Lalique. There is some overlapping of the two periods and some

Vase with moulded design of does and foliage c.1930–35. Sandblasted mark Lalique France. Height 6½in; £1000+.

Paperweight in the shape of a sparrow in clear and etched glass c.1930. Height 3½in; £300–£500.

earlier pieces were marked Lalique and
some later pieces were made using
earlier moulds with the signature R.
Lalique. Modern Lalique glass is
marked Lalique, France.

· LAMPS ·
See Oil Lamps

· LAMPSHADES ·
CEILING AND WALL

Lampshades can be charming and
attractive accessories to the home.
Victorian lampshades were often small
and could be bell-shaped, or four-, six-
or eight-sided. Clear glass shades were
also made in colours of yellow, amber,
dark pink (see CRANBERRY GLASS) and
opalescent glass (see VASELINE GLASS),
and the latter could have the
opalescence attractively ribbed or
whorled. Opaque white shades were
often transfer-printed or hand-painted
with landscapes, scenes of cottage life or
flowers. These small shades could be
either suspended from a central ceiling
rose or attached to a bracket-style wall
light.

Tiffany-style shades (see TIFFANY,
LOUIS COMFORT) which had leaves and
flowers, for example, in a stained-glass
design are prohibitively priced.

The most commonly found shades
dating from the 1920s are usually fairly
large with a shallow, in-turned bowl,

Fan-shaped wall light in
pink/amber glass with
scalloped decoration and
set in a chromed holder
c.1930; £25–£30 for a
single, more for pairs.

1

and were suspended from the ceiling by means of chains. Made in an opaque matt white or coloured glass, they could have a swirling marbled or mottled effect in perhaps yellow, green, pink or blue.

More attractive examples dating from about 1910 had transfer-printed flowers set against an opaque background which was sometimes tinted pink. These were also made in a shallow cone shape and were perhaps decorated with sprays of full-blown roses in pink and yellow, against a delicate tracery of green leaves.

Shades from the 1930s were often made in sets with matching wall lights. They followed the craze for Art Deco styles and were often fan-shaped with a moulded scallop design. The wall light could consist of a single 'fan' set in a chromed holder, while the matching ceiling shade would consist of three fans set together in a holder. The opaque matt shades were made in various shades of white, blue, pink, amber and green.

Square, four-sided shades were also made by inserting oblong strips of glass with angled ends into metal 'shelves'. This gave a stepped or contoured effect, depending on the placing of the metal supports.

LEFT TO RIGHT: Frosted glass shade with frilled edge c.1890.
White glass shade of simple style 19th century.
Small frosted globe for use with an oil lamp.
Green glass shade made in glass in imitation of silk bedroom shade; £10–£20 each.

Ceiling shades from the 1950s could be enormous, sometimes about two or three feet (0.6 to 0.9 m) in diameter, and were round, square or spoked. They tended to be flatter than the earlier 1910–20 shades and were attached to the ceiling by means of a central metal rod rather than chains.

When buying shades that had chain supports it is important to check that the supporting hook inserted into the glass is intact; the chains themselves can be replaced. Victorian shades vary greatly in price from about £15 for small shades in plain colours and of simple style, about £20–£30 for those attractively painted, to about £40–£60 for Cranberry or Vaseline glass examples. Shades from the 1930s which have a mottled effect can still be bought very cheaply at auction for about £5–£10 each; about £15–£20 if the pattern is more attractive. Those dating from about 1910 with a pretty floral pattern can cost as much as £90–£100, although diligent searching can reveal bargains at half that price. Art Deco wall lights of a scalloped fan shape will cost about £20 upwards each, with the matching central light being about £40. Ensure there are no chips to either of these, especially near the chromed fitting. Check also that the chrome is good and not flaking or pitted. Ceiling shades from the 1950s were easily broken and are not often seen, but because of their large size can sometimes be found quite cheaply at boot fairs.

·LEMONADE· ·SETS·

These sets of a jug and six glasses were popular as far back as the 19th century when they were often accompanied by a mirrored or matching glass tray. The glasses were tumbler shaped and the jug was tall. They could be made in pressed or moulded glass (see BLOWN AND BLOW-MOULDED GLASS and PRESS-MOULDED GLASS) in clear, amber, yellow, blue, green or pink glass, and could be plain or enamelled, or have an embossed or rippled pattern.

Lemonade sets from the 1930s and 1950s, however, provide the most scope for the collector. The craze for novelty was at its peak in the 1930s when the Art Deco (q.v.) period flourished. Glasses could be of a trumpet or conical shape, while the jugs were tall, narrow pitchers. Decoration consisted of geometric or abstract designs in red, green, black or silver, or various combinations of these. Bold zig-zags and slashes of vivid colour predominated, as did large penny-sized spots.

Sets from the 1950s can be easily confused with Art Deco styles, but the designs were not quite so stunning and did not have the same quality of verve and style produced by designers of the 1920s and 1930s. Fruit patterns were often painted on to 1950s glass, but whereas Art Deco designers had no hesitation in combining clashing colours such as red/orange/yellow, later designers used these vivid shades individually and so largely lost the intensely dramatic and flamboyant effect of Art Deco.

Over the years tumblers became broken and jugs are separated from the glasses, so to find a complete set in perfect condition is rare. This means that an Art Deco set in good condition with a striking pattern can cost as much as £100-plus. Sets with a jug and four glasses will cost about £80 upwards. Single glasses, however, can be found for about £10–£15 depending on decoration.

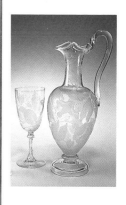

Stourbridge lemonade or water set engraved with a convolvulus design c.1870. Height of jug 14¾in; height of glasses 3½in; £175–£225.

· LUSTRES ·

This term now generally refers to the ornate glass candlesticks of the early 19th century and later mantelpiece ornaments of the Victorian era, although some dealers also refer to the hanging crystal drops as lustres.

Lustres consisted of a goblet- or vase-shaped holder set on a footed stem. The bowl was later adapted into a cup-shaped opening sometimes with an overturned edge or collar, and was fitted with a nozzle for the candle. If used for decorative purposes rather than for illumination, the candle holder was enlarged into a bowl shape which had an outer collar that was plain, frilled or 'V' notched. Small holes were drilled along the edge and tiny hooks of looped metal were inserted. From these were suspended long crystal drops.

The lustres were usually sold in pairs. They were highly ornamental and could be made in opaque white with exquisitely painted decoration in jewel colours which were typical of the Bohemian (q.v.) style. Dark ruby red, rich green and deep blue glass were popular during the Victorian period and these colours could be additionally gilded and/or enamelled with floral patterns, tiny gilt fleurs-de-lys, or scrolled motifs.

The drops were intended to catch and reflect the light, and were often of great length, hanging from the edge of the overturned edge or collar and almost touching the rim of the foot. There were occasionally two rows of drops, one behind the other, and these could be of different colours with clear glass perhaps being set off by ruby drops.

Straight rule drops that resemble faceted oblongs of glass date from about 1840. They were attached by wires to a

Pair of lustres in ruby red glass with triangular faceted drops of slightly alternating length. Height 11in; £400–£600.

large square-faceted crystal which in turn was wired to the bowl of the lustre. More ornate drops consisted of three-sided rules, the side nearest the lustre being notched in curved facets, and the drop terminating in a spear-like point above a narrow 'waist'. Sometimes the drops were pear-shaped, faceted to glitter attractively, and these too are early 19th-century. Icicle drops were 'bomb' shaped and were suspended from wire by one or more faceted beads.

When buying, it is important to check for damage to any frilled or notched parts. The gilding is frequently worn through usage, as is the hand enamelling. The drops are frequently missing or damaged and it can be a tedious task to find an exact match. Check that the missing drops have their wires in the vacant holes and that they are not too badly corkscrewed out of shape.

Pairs of lustres are expensive and examples from the late Victorian era of a large size in a strongly coloured glass will cost about £400–£600 the pair.

The faceted drops can be sought after in their own right. They can be found at antiques fairs for about £1–£1.50 upwards, depending on size and complexity of cutting.

Selection of glass lustre drops; £1–£5 each.

Trademarks were rarely put on glass during the 19th century and most appear on items made in pressed glass (see PRESS-MOULDED GLASS). Unlike registration numbers (see REGISTERED DESIGN NUMBERS) trademarks do not give an exact date of manufacture. Some of the marks were in use over a long period of time, and serve only to identify the manufacturer. Marks were usually placed on the base of the article, but can occasionally be found on an inner surface.

· MAKERS' · TRADEMARKS ·

CLARKE, SAMUEL

Registered in 1876 but in use for fourteen years before this date

1885   FAIRY

1887 (January)

1887 (October)   WEE-FAIRY

Date unknown   CRICKLITE

DAVIDSON, GEORGE & CO

c.1880–90

DERBYSHIRE, JOHN & CO

GALLÉ, EMILE

Stylised signature

GRAY-STAN GLASS

1926+ Used with and
without hyphen

GREENER, HENRY &
CO

1876+

LALIQUE, RENÉ

Etched facsimile script 'R.
Lalique France'

Rare and early moulded
mark used without the 'R'

Moulded 'R. Lalique' mark

MONART GLASS

Paper label c. 1925–30

Paper label c. 1930–61

MONCRIEFF, JOHN

1872+ (Registered in 1876)

SOWERBY'S ELLISON GLASS WORKS

1876+
(Peacock can be found facing both ways)

STEVENS & WILLIAMS
(Brierley Hill)

1886

'THE TAPESTRY GLASSWARE'

1902+

1924+

1926+

1927+

Keith Murray c. 1934–9

Late 1930s

trademarks

TIFFANY GLASS

1905 Favrile Glass

FAVRILE

Mark found on Tiffany's
Favrile Glass

Mark found on Tiffany's
Favrile Glass

Tiffany signature in script
with recorded number pre
1905

Louis C. Tiffany

D1774   L.C.T.

WEBB, THOMAS & SONS

1886 Queen's Burmese
Glass

Mount Washington mark
for Burmese Glass – not to
be confused with the above

1889

1906–35

Webb   *Webb*

1935–49

1950–66

· MARY ·
· GREGORY ·
· GLASS ·

The term Mary Gregory glass refers to the clear and coloured glass that was enamelled with sentimental pictures of Victorian children.

Like Bristol, Nailsea and Sandwich glass (see AMERICAN LACY GLASS, BRISTOL GLASS and NAILSEA GLASS) the term Mary Gregory is generic. There is record of a Mary Gregory who worked at the Boston and Sandwich Glass Factory in Massachusetts between about 1886 and 1888 when the factory closed down, and she did work on the enamelling of glass, but she obviously could not have produced the amount of Mary Gregory glass that is available to collectors.

Mary Gregory glass always includes a child in silhouette, either a boy or a girl, sometimes both together, and they are shown perhaps chasing butterflies, blowing bubbles, fishing, climbing trees, playing a flute, gathering fruit, admiring a flower, or blowing a dandelion clock. The background is often sketchy, with only a landscape of grasses and/or fern-like trees. The girls are usually dressed

Pair of matching jugs in rare turquoise glass, with typical 'Mary Gregory' children depicted in white enamel c.1880. Height 6in; £350–£400.

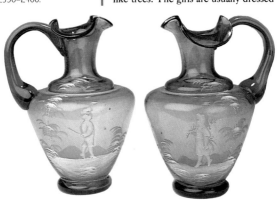

in short, full-skirted dresses, often with a sash or pinafore. The boys wear breeches or knickerbockers with a bloused shirt.

Although clear glass was used for wares, dark red, dark pink (see CRANBERRY GLASS), dark blue and dark green are more frequently encountered. Occasionally, a pale peachy shade can be found, but this is a fairly undistinguished colour. Among the more unusual colours seen are a pale lime or apple green, pale pink (not Cranberry), amethyst, straw yellow and a sharp yellow.

All manner of items were made: beakers and decanters, lemonade sets (q.v.), large and small jugs, sugar and cream sets, and trinket trays (q.v.). Vases were often made in pairs with a girl on one vase and a boy placed in a mirror-image position on the other.

Mary Gregory glass is still being produced today in Bohemia (now Czechoslovakia) and it is important to check the quality of painting, as this is a guide to authenticity. The Victorian figures were enamelled in white, and the brush strokes were light and deft, conveying a feeling of movement and of light and shade in the folds of the children's clothing.

Modern examples show rather crude, lifeless figures with the children less chubby than the Victorian examples. The foreground is rather 'blobby' in execution and the background heavy and dull.

Prices vary quite considerably according to the colour of the glass, with clear and peach being less valuable, and the amount of enamelling. A beaker in Cranberry glass portraying a small girl will be about £50–£60; a small green glass jug portraying a boy at play will be about £60–£70.

m

Ribbed green poison bottles. Height 5½in and 6½in; 50p–£5.

Blue Diuromil bottle complete with glass stopper. Height 5in; £7–£10.

· MEDICINE ·
· & · POISON ·
· BOTTLES ·

Glass bottles have been used for medicines for hundreds of years but it was not until the industrial revolution in the 19th century that they were produced in great quantities for commercial purposes.

Patent medicines were sold with scant regard for accuracy, and elixirs and nostrums were marketed claiming the most extravagant results. Sufferers were assured that Solomon's 'Cordial Balm of Gilead' would relieve them from yellow fever, giving them the promise that they would 'be restored . . . from the jaws of death'. There were remedies, too, for baldness, deafness, rheumatism and lumbago.

There were so many rival products on the market that shrewd businessmen soon realised that the markings on the bottle would make their brand instantly recognisable, and if the bottle was of a different shape, then the novelty factor would also influence the purchase. The traditional shape of the patent medicine bottle was therefore modified by various companies.

H. H. Warner sold his 'Safe Cure' and 'Safe Remedies' in upright rounded bottles that showed a safe moulded in relief (a neat play on words), while Dr Soule's 'Hop Bitters' was sold in a bottle that resembled a small log cabin embellished with hops.

Poison was easily obtainable over the counter and frequent accidents happened with the patient dosing himself from the wrong bottle in error, despite the bottles being made in warning colours of dark cobalt blue, dark green, brown and black. Eventually, a simple solution was found

when the bottles were manufactured with heavy vertical ribbing, or were embossed with warning messages such as the skull-and-crossbones motif. Radam's 'Microbe Killer' was sold in a bottle that showed a man being clubbed by a skeleton, and 'Lysol' disinfectant was sold in a squat bottle with embossed diamond markings. In addition to the ribbing, bottles were also made in square, triangular or many-sided shapes rather than the usual rounded or cylindrical form.

However, some shaped bottles for poison did not prove popular and so the 'wasp-waisted' bottles, for example, were not in production for long, making them collectable. The 'Martin' poison bottle which was intended to lie on its side and which had a 'U'-shaped indentation near the neck, is rare, as are the skull-shaped bottles made in cobalt blue. These were made in three sizes and showed a grinning skull with the word 'Poison' embossed in large letters on its forehead.

The most frequently found patent medicine bottles are those that held hair restoratives. These are readily available for under £10 each, and there is plenty of choice, with Lavona Hair Tonic bottles being only £1, for example. A clear glass bottle that once held Daffy's Elixir will cost £40 upwards, and Robert Turlington's 'Balsam of Life' will be about £30 upwards for a clear bottle.

The ribbed poison bottles in a range of colours are plentiful, and these can be bought for anything between 50p and £5. Those with an indented herringbone pattern will be dearer at about £15–£20. Rare bottles such as the skull will be over £250, and a wasp-waist cobalt blue bottle will be about £200 upwards.

· MIRRORS ·

Apart from being used for examination of one's person, mirrors can give an added dimension to the home, adding reflected light to a gloomy hall perhaps, or highlighting a wall or corner. The manufacture of mirrors or looking-glasses began in England in the 17th century when several Venetian workers were employed in the glasshouses.

The mirrors were first manufactured by splitting blown and shaped sheets of glass (see BLOWN AND BLOW-MOULDED GLASS), but this difficult process soon gave way to a method of casting where large sheets of glass (see WINDOW GLASS) were made by pouring the molten glass on to a flat base. This was then rolled with a metal bar until smooth, when it was given a final polish.

Early glass was silvered with an amalgam of mercury and tin; later processes used real silver or mercury which was protected with a coating of red lead or brown paint. This silvering provided a brilliant reflective surface but was prone to damp and the mercury became dulled over the years.

Quite often the frame was by far the most important part of the mirror and these frames can be found in ornately carved and gilded wood, gesso (a kind

Wall mirror with cream painted frame decorated with gilding and handpainted flowers c.1930/1940. Height 2ft 6in; £45–£70.

of plaster of Paris) and various woods
such as walnut and mahogany.

Victorian mirrors of good quality are
thick and have bevelled edges which fit
into the frame. Overmantel mirrors
were popular and can be found in
mahogany, walnut and ebonised wood.
These were sometimes plain with a
rounded top and were set into a
veneered frame that was sometimes
decorated with a mosaic pattern of
various woods. Other overmantel
mirrors were far more extravagant and
had frames decorated with carved
scrolls. They often had several small
display shelves, each backed by a
mirror, and the overmantel could often
have as many as nine mirrors of various
sizes.

The small dressing mirror was
intended to stand on a chest of drawers
and was an essential part of the dressing
room or bedroom. It was often mounted
in a mahogany frame and supported by
wooden pillars which enabled the mirror
to be tilted. Some mirrors had a shallow
drawer built into the base of the stand.

Edwardian dressing mirrors were
much lighter and more elegant in design
and could be found in round, square or
shield shape.

The free-standing mirror known as a
cheval mirror is a tall, narrow, full-
length mirror supported on a wooden
stand usually made of walnut,
mahogany, satinwood or oak.

Hand mirrors fit into the category of
collectables, and these were usually
once part of a dressing table or travelling
set. Silver-plated or silver-backed
examples were made in round or oval
shape and Victorian hand mirrors can be
found with ornate embossed patterns of
scrolls, leaves and flowers. Winged
cherubs' heads were popular around the
turn of the century, while the

Large barbola mirror with
a decoration of hand-
painted plaster flowers
c.1930. Diameter 12in;
£40–£60.

LEFT: Tin-backed mirror
with embossed pattern.
CENTRE: Two wooden-
backed mirrors.
RIGHT: A wooden-backed
mirror with hand-painted
design; £10–£15 each.

Edwardian period saw a more severe
style with simple patterns carried out in
machine engraving. Wood-backed
mirrors were usually made of ebony or
ebonised wood.

In the 1920s, plastic dressing table
sets were popular and mirrors can be
found in mottled rainbow colours or pale
pastel shades. The 1950s saw hand
mirrors being made with machine-
embroidered backs set in a decorative
metal frame.

When buying mirrors, always check
for chips near the frame. Ensure also
that the silvering is intact, although if
the frame is in good condition and
desirable, the mirror can be resilvered at
a reasonable cost. Thick mirrors are of
better quality than those made of thin
glass. This thickness can be checked by
holding the end of a pencil to the
reflective surface and seeing the gap
between the two; the wider the gap, the
better quality the mirror.

A mahogany dressing mirror from the
Victorian period will cost from about

£40 upwards in good condition, depending on its size, and Edwardian examples are about £50–£80. Cheval mirrors are desirable and a Queen Anne reproduction style dating from about 1910 will be about £150–£200. Those made in oak in the 1930s can sometimes be found at auction for about £40 upwards.

Overmantel mirrors will vary in price between about £30–£40 for a plain variety found in auction, to about £150–£250 for one of larger size with many shelves.

Hand mirrors in silver can be costly, and those with heavily embossed patterns will start at about £60–£90; silver-plated mirrors are much cheaper, but ensure that the plating is good and not worn or yellowed. Plastic-framed hand mirrors start at about £5, as do those from the 1950s.

· MONART ·
· GLASS ·

Moncrieff Ltd had been in the glass manufacturing business in Perth since about 1865 when they made glass for engineering and chemical works. But the post-war slump in 1918 led to new avenues being explored and in 1924 the production of art glass began. It was a joint venture between Mrs Moncrieff and a family of Spanish glassblowers named Ysart. At first, just Salvador, the father, and Paul, his eldest son, worked for the Moncrieffs, but they were later joined by Salvador's other sons, Antoine, Vincent and Augustine.

The 'Scotch' glass, as it was called, was made until the advent of World War II when production was suspended. After that, in 1946, Paul Ysart began production on his own for the Moncrieffs, and it is generally agreed

Bulbous vase in green with gold 'splashing'. Height 5in; £100–£150.

that 1939 saw the end of Monart glass as such. The other members of the Ysart family had left Moncrieff's by then and opened their own factory in order to manufacture Vasart Glass, the name being made up from the initial letters of Vincent, Augustine and Salvador (Antoine having been killed in a road accident) and the 'art' from Ysart.

Monart glass usually consisted of three layers. The first gather of glass would be rolled on to a layer of crushed, coloured enamels which were then worked in. A final casing of clear glass was added before the piece was blown and worked. The enamel colours were often mixed or 'pulled' into patterns of swirling whorls. Alternatively, the glass was given an added texture by using crushed enamels on the final surface before blowing.

A type of cased glass called 'Cloisonne' was made by rolling the crystal-cased coloured gather in crushed white enamel. After fusing the white enamel by reheating, the glass was plunged into cold water, causing the outer casing to crack. When the glass was then blown into shape, the cracks widened into gaps, showing the bottom layer of colour beneath the central crystal casing. After further working, the

A Monart vase in swirling amber glass giving a latticinio effect c.1935. Height 14in; £300–£500.

piece was exposed to sulphur fumes and the white enamel took on a metallic lustre.

Other techniques included randomly placed and variously sized bubbles as a pattern in the glass, and the factory developed a striped and ribbed method of patterning which produced a latticinio effect. In the 1930s small flakes of gold or aventurine gave an interesting flecked appearance, while silver flecks were more simply achieved by using packets of silver frosting from Woolworth's.

Vase in swirling pattern of blue, green and brown glass c.1920. Height 8in; £400–£500.

The factory made mainly flower vases and holders, and bowls, although pendant light shades and table lamps were also produced.

Monart glass can be difficult to recognise as the manufacturers' practice was to apply a paper label to the surface of the finished product, and this has often been lost over the years (see MAKERS' TRADEMARKS). As Monart glass was frequently of a less fine quality than other glass of a similar nature, it will not ring clearly when lightly tapped but will respond with a dull ringing sound. For further identification, the collector will need to refer to a published catalogue of Monart shapes. There were 312 recorded shapes of different sizes and the catalogue is a useful guide.

Prices will vary according to the piece and complexity of design. A large vase of about 14 inches (35 cm) in height and made in blue and green enamels will cost about £400–£500. A smaller vase coloured in pink, green and white will be about £150–£175.

· MOULDED ·
· GLASS ·
See Blown and Blow-Moulded Glass

Clear glass hip flask with opaque white looping c.1860. Length 7in; £100–£125.

· NAILSEA ·
· GLASS ·

The Nailsea Glasshouse, near Bristol, was established by John Robert Lucas in 1788. The factory made bottle glass and crown window glass (see WINDOW GLASS) and, because of the heavy excise duty on fine lead glass, the factory manufactured a non-lead soda lime glass to avoid or lessen the burden of taxation.

The bottles were of dark glass, green or green/brown, blackish green and a green with a yellow/brown tinge. By comparison, the window glass was a clear pale green, the colour coming from the impurities in the sand that was found near the village of Nailsea.

Some domestic wares were made, such as jugs, carafes, flasks, large cream separators for the dairy, and lace-makers' lamps (q.v.). These items were all made in pale green glass but this colour is sometimes hard to detect and can often only be seen where the glass is thicker, near the handles of jugs, for example, or at the base. Some 'friggers' (q.v.) or novelty pieces were also made at Nailsea, but specific attribution cannot be made to these items.

The glassmakers added decoration to the plain pieces by applying white and coloured enamels. Sometimes the pieces were 'marvered' with small flecks and

LEFT: Pale green water jug in crown window glass with opaque white trailing around rim c.1810. Height 8¾in; £400–£600.
RIGHT: Olive green bottle glass water jug with coloured marvered inclusions, sometimes known as Wrockwardine glass. Height 9½in; £600–£700.

LEFT: Crown window glass jug with opaque white marvered inclusions and white trailed rim c.1800. Height 4½in; £350–£450.
RIGHT: Bonnet glass in dark green bottle glass with white marvered inclusions c.1780. Height 3½in; £120–£170.

chips of contrasting enamel. This process involved rolling the item, still attached to the punty rod, on to a hard surface. The still-molten glass would pick up the blobs of scattered glass and, as the rolling continued, these would be absorbed into the body of the piece giving it a mottled or speckled appearance. This glass is known as 'speckled', 'splashed' or 'splatter' glass.

Another form of decoration was to adorn the piece with trails of opaque white glass; sometimes other colours were used such as pink, red, blue and yellow. The additional threads of glass were looped or combed across the surface using a pointed tool, a technique first practised by the Egyptians from about 1500 BC and later by the Romans. (See also NAILSEA-STYLE GLASS.)

· NAILSEA-STYLE · · GLASS ·

The term 'Nailsea' is now considered to be generic for a number of decorative and novelty items (see FRIGGERS) that were produced in the late 18th and 19th centuries by glasshouses in the Bristol and surrounding areas, and in the Midlands and Scotland also.

One of the characteristics of Nailsea-style glass is the looped trails of opaque white or coloured glass that decorated

Blue cream jug with opaque white looping and clear handle and foot c.1860. Height 3½in; £175–£225.

Snuff jar with folded rim
c.1810. Height 10¼in;
£120–£150.

Two-compartmented
Nailsea-style gimmel flask
with white and pink
looping c.1860. Length
9in; £100–£150.

the pieces. These loops or festoons were sometimes combed while still plastic, giving a softer, all-over appearance to the pattern. The looped patterns were frequently applied to flasks, carafes, jugs, rolling pins, witch balls and pipes (see ROLLING PINS; PIPES; and WITCH BALLS). Perhaps the best recognised example is the double flask or 'gimmel' flask. It is thought that this flask with its long curved double opening was intended to be used as a cruet, possibly for holding oil and vinegar.

Apart from the combed and looped work, spirals and stripes of glass were also used decoratively on glass, and walking sticks (q.v.) can be found with inner twisted spirals of red, blue and white glass. This threaded work is commonly known as latticinio, the term being derived from the Venetians who used the technique to great effect in the 16th century and later.

Nailsea-style glass was also 'splashed' with blobs of contrasting glass, giving it a mottled or speckled appearance. The piece that was to be so decorated was 'marvered' or rolled on to a hard surface while still plastic. The small blobs of white or coloured glass that had been placed there would be picked up and absorbed into the still-molten glass during this rolling process, giving it its characteristic appearance. This type of glass is also known as 'splatter' glass.

Nailsea-type glass was made at several factories in the Bristol area. It was also made at Stourbridge, Sunderland, Newcastle, Warrington, Wrockwardine Wood, and Alloa in Scotlan

· NORTHWOOD ·
JOHN (1836–1902)
He was first employed by Richardson's (q.v.), a firm of glassmakers, in 1848

where he learned the techniques of painting, enamelling and gilding, and began his experiments with cameo carving (see CAMEO GLASS).

He left the company in 1852 to work with his elder brother, and in 1860 they established a successful decorating business. In 1880, John Northwood was offered the post of art director for Stevens & Williams (q.v.) which he accepted while still carrying on his own business.

In about 1856, Northwood produced his first piece of cameo glass, and in 1873, after eight years' work, he engraved the Elgin Vase, the relief design based on a frieze taken from the Elgin Marbles. There had always been interest in the famous Portland Vase (see CAMEO GLASS) and this was renewed in 1845 after the vase had been smashed and then restored. Glassmakers regarded it as a challenge, and Benjamin Richardson offered a prize of £1000 to the first man who could successfully make an accurate copy. In 1873, Northwood began work on the blank of a vase produced by his cousin, Philip Pargeter, using both the traditional engraver's tools and acid for etching. The vase was completed three years later and Northwood won the prize. Unfortunately, shortly after its manufacture, John Northwood held the vase in his warm hands on a frosty morning, and the vase cracked due to the contrast in temperature.

John Northwood went on to produce more fine pieces, including one for Webb's (q.v.) and, together with his son, also named John, established a school for cameo carving. His techniques firmly established the use of acid-etching in cameo work and led to a 25-year period of popularity for the carved glass.

O

· OIL · LAMPS ·

The history of the oil lamp goes back to the 18th century. At first it gave a poor light, flickering badly and smoking, but in 1784 Amie Argand invented a round burner with a tubular wick. It was later found that the addition of a glass chimney gave extra brilliance to the light. The use of refined paraffin as fuel in the early 19th century gave the oil lamp a boost, and when Joseph Hinks invented the Duplex burner with its double wick in 1865, this form of lighting was well and truly established.

The oil lamp consists of four parts: the base containing the reservoir (known as the fount) for paraffin, the wick and carrier, a clear glass chimney, and a glass shade.

The base could be made of metal (brass or cast iron), ceramic or glass, and was often very decorative. Ceramic bases sometimes resembled vases and were finely painted. Glass bases were made in various colours such as dark blue, dark green or pink (see CRANBERRY GLASS). If of clear glass, they would be cut in diamond patterns (see CUTTING, GLASS).

The shades were of a round or tulip shape. Sometimes they were plain globes of opaque white glass, or were frosted, etched or cut. More desirable examples were frilled at the top opening and these could be of clear glass, etched in elaborate patterns of scrolls, flowers and/or acanthus leaves. Coloured glass was also used, in both opaque and clear glass, and the most sought-after shades are Cranberry and Vaseline glass (q.v.). If the base was of glass, then the shade was often made to match.

Various lamps were made for different functions. The tall vase-shaped lamp was intended for use on the table;

Tall oil lamp with white glass base c.1890–1900.
Height 1ft 10in; £45–£60.

a more squat version sat on the sideboard. There were also small bracket lamps which were attached to the front of a piano, larger ones which were set on the wall, and hanging lamps for the hallway.

When buying, it is important to check that the oil lamp is not a reproduction. If the base is cast iron, check the underside for any roughness in the casting; Victorian lamps were finished off more smoothly than their modern counterparts. Check brass lamps also; modern brass is thinner than old brass, and more 'brassy' in colour.

Wick carriers should be carefully checked if it is intended that the lamp should be used. Ensure that there is no damage and that the action is smooth. Replacement chimneys can be obtained from specialist dealers for a few pounds.

A brass lamp with a Cranberry shade will cost about £150–£200, as will one made in Vaseline glass. A coloured opaque glass lamp with matching shade and some enamelling will be about £80–£150. A squat sideboard lamp will cost from about £30–£40 upwards depending on the style and ornamentation.

Small oil lamp with clear glass base and carrying handle. Height 10in; £20–£30.

· OPAL · & · OPALINE · GLASS ·

This term applies to the semi-opaque translucent glass that was partly or wholly opacified by adding agents such as tin oxide or calcium phosphate (bone-ash). When white, the glass has an appearance similar to that of soft white alabaster. It was also made in delicate colours of yellow, turquoise, blue, green and a reddish pink, and some glass had a mauve tinge. These colours were often seen in a marbled pattern. Black

Opaline white goblet with black transfer desert scene and vitrified enamel colours c.1850, marked Richardsons. Height 6½in, £275–£325.

Cream jug and sugar basin in rare blue/green opaline with cold enamelled decoration in pristine condition c.1840. Height 4½in and 4¾in; £425–£475.

opaline was also made.

A speciality of the French factories was 'gorge de pigeon' (pigeon's neck) which was a delicate greyish mauve, and 'bulles de savon' (soap bubbles) which had a delightful rainbow appearance to the glass. Opal was the word first used and this is generally applied to English glass. The word opaline came later, in the 20th century, although 'opalin' was mentioned by Baccarat in France in the early 1800s, when it was used mainly to describe glass of French origin.

A wide variety of items were made, such as vases, lamp bases and candlesticks, carafes, scent bottles (q.v.) and sweetmeat baskets. These were often painted or enamelled, and sometimes the paintings were embellished with coloured enamel pellets which gave a jewelled effect.

French glass of an early period is prohibitively priced, and beyond the average collector. However, later English examples can be found for about £40–£60 for a small vase with limited decoration.

· OPAQUE ·
· WHITE · GLASS ·

This creamy white glass was first manufactured by the Egyptians when it was known as milk-and-water glass. The technique was later revived in the 1760s

O

when clear glass was coloured with arsenic or tin oxide to produce a glass that was intended to imitate porcelain. The Germans called it 'milchglas' or 'porzellanglas', and when used as threaded glass by the Venetians it was known as 'latticinio' (from the Italian 'latte' meaning milk). The glass was often gilded, or enamelled in transparent polychrome colours.

Decoration on the glass in the 18th century was very finely done. Flowers were delicately copied, and were often accompanied by butterflies and/or birds, such as the goldfinch, which were realistically portrayed. By the 19th century, however, mass production techniques had taken over from the skilled painters and enamellers.

Victorian vases can be easily found, and these are often decorated with bouquets of flowers and leaves. The standard of this painting can vary enormously, and some examples are quite poor with drab colours and too-heavy strokes making the piece unattractive. Occasionally one can find a landscape painted with delicate brushwork and pleasant colours.

When buying, ensure that the painting on the piece is in good condition and is not worn or rubbed. A late-Victorian vase of reasonable size will cost about £30–£40 upwards depending on the quality of the painting. Early 18th-century glass will be prohibitively expensive.

Egg cup with translucent amethyst rim c.1830. Height 3¼in; £125–£175.

Rare opaque white English vase with enamelled chinoiserie decoration c.1780. Height 5¼in; £2000+.

· ORREFORS ·

This Swedish glassworks was established in 1898. In 1916, the company turned to the production of art glass (q.v.) and engaged two designers of note, Simon Gate and Edward Hald. When the new-style glass was displayed

O

20th century Orrefors glass beakers with engraved designs c.1955–65; £20–£50.

Orrefors decanter engraved with female figure and marked 'Adam Och Eva', 20th century; £100–£200.

at the Paris Exhibition of 1925 it was an immediate success.

Orrefors' Graal glass which had been developed over the years was something new and exciting. Basically, it was cased glass (see CAMEO GLASS) but instead of being finished off by engraving and etching on the cold glass, the designers achieved their effects by placing it in a furnace. This gave the pattern a fluidity of motion which complemented the naturalistic patterns.

Another technique was that of providing designs by means of inlaid air bubbles. Figures and scenes appeared almost etched or engraved into the glass. This technique was known as Ariel.

The Swedish glass was also engraved. The delicate patterns contrasted well with the clear heavy glass. Apart from Graal and Ariel and their fine engraved glass, Orrefors was noted for the depth of colour produced in the mosaic and inlaid glass that was made in the 1940s. It was named Ravenna after the mosaic and stained glass that graced the cathedral at Ravenna in Italy.

Orrefors glass can be extremely expensive. For example, a signed Graal bowl showing galloping horses will cost over £500. By contrast, however, a small perfume bottle dating from the 1950s, signed and having an engraved galleon as decoration, will cost only about £30–£4

paperweights

Despite the fact that the origin of glass goes back to the ancient Egyptians, paperweights were not manufactured until the mid-19th century. Their collectability is of comparatively recent origin, too, as it was not until a major auction of paperweights took place in 1952 that these attractive items were brought to public notice.

The first and most finely executed weights were made by the French factories of Baccarat, Clichy and Saint-Louis, although some sources credit the origin of millefiori weights to an Italian glassmaker named Pietro Bigaglia. Apsley Pellatt made crystal cameo weights in England, as did John Ford in Edinburgh, and millefiori weights were produced in the Stourbridge area.

By the middle of the century, paperweights were also being made in America by factories such as the Boston and Sandwich Glass Works, and the Mount Washington Glass Works.

· TYPES · OF · · PAPERWEIGHTS ·

These fall roughly into three categories: millefiori, sulphide, and subject weights.

Millefiori means, literally, a thousand flowers, and these weights were made by fusing together long coloured-glass rods into a floral pattern. This multi-coloured rod would then be sliced in rounds, and set out decoratively in tightly packed rows or spacious garland patterns held together by molten glass. The 'design' would be picked up by a small blob or 'gather' of clear glass held by the glassmaker on his pontil rod. The gather was then dipped into molten glass before being rolled in a wooden cup kept cool with water. This rolling gave the paperweight a domed shape which magnified the pattern made by the millefiori canes. When the canes were set in a rising pattern, they were known as 'mushroom' weights.

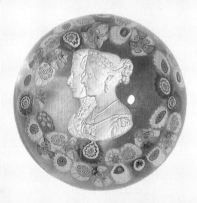

Paperweight with sulphide profiles of a young Victoria and Albert, with millefiori canes, made to commemorate their wedding in 1840; £900–£1000+.

Additional decoration was added in the form of latticinio, where threads of opaque white glass were criss-crossed or swirled across the base of the weight to give an attractive background to the flower or fruit patterns.

The manufacture of sulphides was pioneered by James Tassie of Glasgow in the 18th century when he made small medallions of china clay, or glass paste. In 1819 Sir Apsley Pellatt patented his 'crystallo-ceramie' for making cameos. These were made from a vitreous paste which resembled porcelain, and by 1831 Pellatt was setting them into clear crystal paperweights. A curved layer of clear glass magnified the portraits.

Subject weights were made in style similar to millefiori weights but were inlaid with flowers, fruit, insects or snakes.

Paperweights could be additionally decorated by slicing 'windows' or 'printies', as they were called in the trade, into the domed glass at the top and sides. This gave an extra dimension to the interior pattern. Occasionally, a layer of coloured glass would be added before this faceting was done, and these paperweights were known as overlay weights (see CAMEO GLASS).

· AMERICAN ·
· PAPERWEIGHTS ·

The Americans began making paperweights around 1850 and were heavily influenced by French and English glassmakers. However, a few glasshouses developed their own distinctive styles.

Large dark green glass 'dump' or doorstop weight made by J. Kilner of Wakefield c.1855. Impressed seal. £90–£100.

Perthshire millefiori weight set with white, blue and pink canes, and orange, green and white twisted ribbons on a green cushion c.1960. The maker's signature 'P' is at the top of the pictured weight; £30–£50.

The New England Glass Company in Cambridge, Massachusetts, specialised in weights which contained glass fruit and their flower weights contained designs representing blooms such as the yellow clematis, the buttercup and a brilliant red poinsettia, while the Sandwich glassworks (The Boston and Sandwich Glass Co) was famed for its flower weights, some containing upright floral bouquets.

William Gillinder (Gillinder & Sons), an English glassmaker who had settled in America, produced paperweights with a distinctive high dome and deep oval printies. The factory also produced moulded bird and animal weights in clear, opaque white or black glass.

The Mount Washington Glass Co became famous for their 'Mount Washington Roses'. These were large weights, some four and a half inches (11 cm) in diameter, which contained single blooms of full-blown roses, often accompanied by unrealistic butterflies. They also made weights containing flowers and fruits.

Roses in weights were also produced by Whitall Tatum & Co at Millville, New Jersey, but their rose was an upright, sculpted bloom. They favoured the lily, too, and this was seen with ribs of red, blue and green glass. Their speciality was a small, clear faceted paperweight which contained a sailing ship. Most of their upright weights stood on a footed base.

· FRENCH · PAPERWEIGHTS ·

The three main factories were those of Baccarat, Clichy and Saint-Louis.

Baccarat, a leading glasshouse, began producing paperweights in about 1846. But production was short-lived and lasted only until

Modern Chinese paperweight with red amaryllis flower set in clear glass. Diameter 3in; £15–£25.

Clear glass paperweight with tinted photographic print of St. Leonards-on-Sea. Late Victorian; £15–£25.

about 1849, although the renewed interest in paperweights in the 1950s saw a revival of the industry.

Many of the Baccarat weights are identifiable by the letter 'B' set at the side. This is usually accompanied by the date of manufacture, and the most commonly seen dates are those for 1847 and 1848. The base was sometimes decorated by a distinctive star cutting.

Typical Baccarat weights show flower centres made of a whorl of glass in 'swiss roll' style surrounded by a star cluster formation. A broad-arrow floret (pointing inwards) is also attributed to Baccarat. Canes bearing finely made animal silhouettes were a feature of the glasshouse; more rare was the 'red' or 'dancing devil', which was used as a central motif. Since 1958 all the weights made contain silhouette canes showing the signs of the zodiac. This makes it easier to identify the modern weights and not to confuse them with the antique weights.

The Clichy glasshouse was situated at Clichy-la-Garenne on the outskirts of Paris. Production started there in about 1839, and the glasshouse soon gained a reputation for excellence. The production of paperweights began in about 1846 and continued until about 1870. The glasshouse is best known for the 'Clichy Rose', a many-petalled flower usually made in white or pink. Some weights contained the letter 'C' in the centre of the weight. This can be mistaken for a horseshoe and is often overlooked. Very few weights have the name Clichy in full.

With 400 years of glassmaking to its credit, the glasshouse of Saint-Louis in Lorraine had achieved an enviable reputation for fine glass. Like Baccarat and Clichy, the factory produced paperweights from 1845 until 1860, and some of the weights were signed 'SL'. Among their specialities were the jasper ground weights. They were often designed to show panels of jasper (partially pulverised glass)

Lalique paperweight, 'Chouette', in the shape of an owl, made in clear and etched glass and mounted on a cylindrical base c.1930. Height 3½in; £300–£500.

and green, separated by spokes of white in a wheel formation. Another speciality was the crown weight, which consisted of a hollow glass globe into which were set twisted threads or ribbons of glass. These weights often have a hole at the base. The Saint-Louis canes are lighter in colour than those of Baccarat and Clichy, and the paperweights themselves are rounder and taller.

· ENGLISH ·
· PAPERWEIGHTS ·

Bacchus (Bacchus & Sons) seem to have been the only glasshouse with a documented record of paperweight making, although the Islington Glassworks (also in Birmingham) is thought to have made them. Bacchus began producing their 'letterweights' in about 1848, and showed them at a Birmingham Exhibition in 1849. The weights were in the French style but were large, usually over three inches (7 cm) in diameter, with a narrow base.

Paperweights were also made by James Powell's company, Whitefriars, from about 1848, and these were of the millefiori type. The weights were flat based and had either a low dome, or a slightly higher dome after the French style. A more rare weight had a very high dome with straight sides and a footed rim.

Bottle glass weights or 'dumps' were made in various factories throughout the country as 'friggers' (q.v.) by the workmen at the end of the day. These high-domed weights varied in size, from a small weight of about four inches (10 cm) in height to a huge version which was intended for use as a door stop.

The dumps were built up by adding successive layers of glass to the marver. Enclosed in these layers were large air bubbles that resembled fountains or tears, and strange plant-like forms. These larger bubbles were, in turn, surrounded by a mass of tiny silvery bubbles. This effect was achieved by combining chalk dust with the hot molten glass during production, the action of the heat giving off gaseous bubbles of varying sizes.

· SOUVENIR · WEIGHTS ·

These are perhaps the most affordable of paperweights for the small collector. They could be of either a round, flattened form, or ovals or oblongs of clear glass with rounded or bevelled corners. Affixed to the base of the paperweight was a transfer printing of a coloured view of a holiday resort, usually a seaside town such as Brighton or Clacton-on-Sea, for example. Churches and notable or historic buildings were also popular. Later, sepia photographs or transfers replaced the coloured drawings. The back of the picture was often left unprotected and many of the scenes have been damaged over the years.

·PEARLINE· ·GLASS·

This was the trade name given to an opaque glass developed by the firm of George Davidson & Co (q.v.) in 1889. An advertisement in the 'Pottery Gazette' described the new glass which had first been made in a pale turquoise colour: 'The base is in a rich blue and the edge is of a paler colour, to which the name "Pearline" is most appropriate.'

The glass was later produced in primrose, a rather strong acid yellow with creamy overtones. This is often mistakenly called Vaseline glass (q.v.) but the colour is stronger than that of Vaseline glass and more opaque and dense in appearance.

Pearline was made in pressed glass (see PRESS-MOULDED GLASS) and achieved its opacity by being reheated once pressed. The longer and more intense the heat, the greater was the degree of opacity. It was used for making all sorts of items: cream and sugar sets, butter dishes, tazzas, biscuit boxes, celery vases, water sets, sweetmeat baskets, and so on.

Pearline glass can be readily found at antiques fairs, and is often marked with a registered number (see REGISTERED DESIGN NUMBERS). Before buying, check for any chips and cracks.

Tazza in turquoise pearline glass made by George Davidson and marked with registered design number for 1889. Diameter 7½in; £50–£75.

Decorative feet on the base were often composed of several 'leaves' of glass and these are prone to damage. Cracks can be obscured in a heavily patterned piece.

A small cream and sugar set will cost about £40–£50 upwards, and a sweetmeat basket will be about the same price, depending on the size, shape and pattern.

·PIANO·RESTS·

These rather strange-looking objects were made in the mid-19th century, from 1860 until about 1915, and are often mistaken for paperweights or

ashtrays. The Victorians knew them by several different names: piano feet or stands, pianoforte insulators or inductors. The rests were intended to support the feet of the piano, the theory being that glass was a good conductor and that the sound of the music would become more resonant. They were originally made in sets of four for an upright piano, although only three would be used for a grand piano.

Piano rests were made by a number of manufacturers but are rarely marked with the maker's name (see MAKERS' TRADEMARKS) or a registered number (see REGISTERED DESIGN NUMBERS). They are basically large lumps of pressed or moulded glass which had central indentations to take the piano feet, and shapes varied from the flattish round 'jelly mould' style to heavy square

Piano rests made in clear glass and in black glass; £3–£10.

p

blocks for the grand piano. They were made in clear glass and in colours such as green (various), dark blue, amber, an acid yellow, black and a rich turquoise. More rarely, they were made in Vaseline glass (q.v.).

As many people are ignorant of their use, piano rests can still be found at bargain prices, and the collector can get away with paying as little as £3 or £4 for each one. At an antiques fair, however, the piano rests will be double that price. Complete sets are rarely found and so will be priced accordingly. Good hunting grounds are junk shops and flea markets.

Long Nailsea style pipe with hollow bobbin stem c.1860. Length 18in; £150–£175.

The bowl of a pale green pipe of barley sugar twist design; £100–£150.

· PIPES ·

These were made for purely ornamental purposes and were often blown in ornate and bizarre shapes. They are generally regarded as 'friggers' (q.v.) and were made by the workmen at the end of the day's work to demonstrate their skill in glassmaking.

The pipe invariably had a long curved stem and this was decorated with a varying number of blown 'chambers' before it met the bowl. A few were made in plain coloured glass such as dark blue, a deep turquoise, ruby or green, but the majority seem to have been made in the Nailsea style (see NAILSEA GLASS and NAILSEA-STYLE GLASS) when green, pink and blue glass was ornamented by combed loops and stripes of white glass.

As the pipes were delicate and easily damaged, they are not often found. Prices are therefore high and a clear ruby pipe from the mid-19th century will cost in the region of £150–£200 or more.

· PRESS-MOULDED ·
· GLASS ·

The technique of pressing glass by hand or machine, as opposed to free blowing or blow moulding (see BLOWN AND BLOW-MOULDED GLASS), originated in America in the early 19th century, although it had been used in a limited manner in England in the 18th century. Pressed glass was necessarily heavier than blown or blow-moulded glass and the heavy duty payable on glass by weight in England delayed any development. However, this tax was abolished in 1845 and press-moulded glass came into its own.

The glass was made by using two moulds, an inner and an outer. The molten metal was put into the mould, then the inner mould, piston or plunger, would be inserted using a lever system for added pressure. This forced the glass into the mould and produced patterns of a sharp crispness. It also enabled articles to be produced which had a pattern either on the inner or outer surface of the piece, or on both inner and outer surfaces.

The process was ideally suited to the making of bowls or vases, but the use of the plunger made it impossible to produce items which were wider at the base than the top. Decanters, therefore, were made in two halves, top and bottom, both moulds being hinged together. Once the shapes were pressed on and the plunger removed, the mould holding the upper part of the decanter

Two-piece flower block possibly by George Davidson showing a seated girl with a parasol, set on a perforated base c.1920/30. Height 8½in, £25–£40.

Cream jug with fluted pattern and bearing registered design number for 1887. Height 4in; £10–£20.

Opalescent glass fish with the opalescence appearing gold against the light. Made in France and marked Sabino. Height 2½in; £30–£50.

would be swung on to the base, ensuring that the two parts would 'marry' while the glass was still hot. The outer moulds were then removed.

The moulds for pressed glass were made in cast iron or gunmetal and occasionally brass, and were in two, three or four hinged parts. As so much pressure was applied to these moulds, the molten glass forced its way into the slight gaps, creating seam lines. These were often removed by fire polishing.

The method of manufacture enabled the glassmakers to mark their goods and much pressed glass carries a trademark and/or registered design number (see MAKERS' TRADEMARKS and REGISTERED DESIGN NUMBERS).

Initially, press-moulded glass copied the styles and patterns of cut glass, but gradually manufacturers patented new designs and colours. Opaque glass (see VITRO-PORCELAIN GLASS) in both plain and marbled colours proved popular, and a huge variety of articles were made ranging from the purely domestic, such as butter dishes, cream and sugar sets, plates and other tableware, to small posy holders and sweetmeat dishes in novelty shapes, such as miniature coal trucks, rowing boats, boots and shoes (see SHOES AND BOOTS), baskets (q.v.) and swans. Ornaments and paperweights were produced in designs of Punch and Judy, Britannia, a sphinx, dogs, and lions based on those at the base of Nelson's Column designed by Landseer. Commemorative items (q.v.), generally plates and beakers, were also made in clear, amber or green pressed glass, and these can be found marking Queen Victoria's Golden and Diamond Jubilees and later coronations.

Pressed glass ham stand with diamond moulding and toothed rim c.1880. Height 7½in; £40–£60.

r

·REGISTERED·
·DESIGN·
·NUMBERS·

Between 1842 and 1883 much pressed glass (see PRESS-MOULDED GLASS) was made bearing a diamond-shaped registry mark. This meant that the design had been protected by registering it with the Patent Office Design Registry in London. The diamond was marked with the class of goods – glass was III, ceramics were IV – the day, month and year of registration, and the parcel or bundle number. The original diamond was changed in 1868 so that the date letters appeared in different places. A key to both diamonds is shown below.

Index to year letters for 1842–67 (year letter at top)

A	1845	B	1858	C	1844
D	1852	E	1855	F	1847
G	1863	H	1843	I	1846
J	1854	K	1857	L	1856
M	1859	N	1864	O	1862
P	1851	Q	1866	R	1861
S	1849	T	1867	U	1848
V	1850	W	1865	X	1842
Y	1853	Z	1860		

DIAMOND USED BETWEEN
1842–67

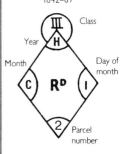

Index to year letters for 1868–83 (year letter at right)

A	1871	C	1870	D	1878
E	1881	F	1873	H	1869
I	1872	J	1880	K	1883
L	1882	P	1877	S	1875
U	1874	V	1876	X	1868
Y	1879				

*The letter W was used as the year letter from 1–6 March 1878.

DIAMOND USED BETWEEN
1868–83

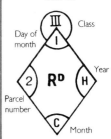

r

*The month letter R was used between 1–19 September 1857, and the letter K was used for December 1860. From 1–16 March 1878 the letter G was used for the month.

· DESIGN ·
· REGISTRATIONS ·

The system of protecting designs began in 1842 with official registration. In 1883 there was an amalgamation of categories in which glass, ceramics, metal etc. were all grouped together into Class 4, and this system was put into operation in January 1884. The manufactured article was marked with a series of numbers which were sometimes accompanied by the prefix Reg No or Rd No. These numbers will give the date of registration of the design and will also, in most cases, identify the manufacturer.

Design registration numbers from 1884

1884	1	**1893**	205240
1885	19754	**1894**	224720
1886	40480	**1895**	246975
1887	64520	**1896**	268392
1888	90483	**1897**	291241
1889	116648	**1898**	311658
1890	141273	**1899**	331707
1891	163767	**1900**	351202
1892	185713	**1901**	368154

(See also MAKERS' TRADEMARKS.)

· RICHARDSONS ·
THE

The name Richardson appears in several guises in the Midlands glass industry and refers to three brothers, William Hayden, Benjamin and Jonathan Richardson. William and Benjamin first went into partnership with Thomas Webb (q.v.). In 1836, the partnership was dissolved and the brothers, with the addition of Jonathan, formed their own company, W. H., B. & J. Richardson. Benjamin later ran Richardsons' alone, with his son Henry taking over towards the end of the 1800s.

The firm became known for its clear glass products which were attractively enamelled in floral patterns. They were among the first manufacturers of pressed glass (see PRESS-MOULDED GLASS) and were also noted for the manufacture of Rusticana, decorative glass holders which took the form of tree trunks with twig-like branches and small feet shaped like roots (see VASELINE GLASS).

All three brothers were skilled glassmakers but it was Benjamin Richardson (1802–87) who became known as the 'Father of the Glass Trade'. He is credited with the invention of a glass-threading machine which reduced the time in applying threaded glass to decorative items. He also introduced a wide range of coloured glass, producing new colours such as topaz and a vivid green. He experimented with the process of etching on glass and was greatly interested in the carving of glass, offering a prize of £1000 in 1860 to the first glassmaker who produced a copy of the Portland Vase (see CAMEO GLASS and NORTHWOOD, JOHN).

Water jug with green and white lily decoration and marked 'Richardsons vitrified enamel colours' and having lozenge mark for 1848. Height 9½in; £700–£900.

Green goblet with gilt decoration and hollow ringed foot c.1850. Marked 'Richardsons Stourbridge'. Height 5in. £180–£220.

r

Two Nailsea style pins with blue and white, and pink and white looping c.1860. Length 17in and 17½in respectively; £80–£100 and £80–£90.

Olive green pin in Nailsea style with blue and yellow marvered inclusions c.1810; £45–£60.

· ROLLING ·
· PINS ·

These were made from the early 18th century onwards and throughout the 19th century, and early examples can be found in pale green crown or window glass (see NAILSEA GLASS and WINDOW GLASS). The rolling pins fall into the class of novelties or 'friggers' (q.v.) and were made largely for ornamental use, although they were also used for practical purposes.

The pins were made with rounded knob-like ends and occasionally one of these would be stoppered with a cork, making the pin into a container. Some of those made at Nailsea held exactly 1 lb (0.45 kg) of tea. Other rolling pins were filled with sugar or with salt to give them weight and keep them cool for pastry making. These were often hung with a beadwork handle and placed above a fireplace for decoration and to keep the contents dry.

Many were made in dark blue Bristol glass (q.v.) and were decorated with gilding. Some rolling pins were elaborately enamelled with flowers such as roses or had transfer-printed designs on them. Nailsea-style (q.v.) rolling pins were decorated with combed loops of pink, red or blue against an opaque white ground.

Glass rolling pins were favourite gifts with sailors who gave them to their wives or sweethearts as love tokens. These can be found decorated with paintings of ships, and/or verses such as 'Love the Giver'. A typical verse is: 'When I am far upon the sea, Bear me in your mind. Let the world say what they may, Speak of me as you find.'

Pins made in Sunderland carried views of the Wear Bridge and a plea to 'Forget Me Not'. Decoration on the

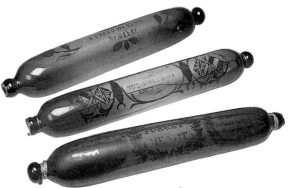

r

latter was often 'etched' into the glass in a series of small dots by using a hardened tool. Oil paints were then added to the design before the rolling pin was gently refired.

Cut-out patterns were used successfully inside the rolling pins. These coloured prints of figures and animals were pasted on to the interior of the glass before it was gilded. Alternatively, the cut-outs were pasted on to a long solid tube of plaster which was then encased in clear glass.

Often the transfer printing or oil painting has worn badly over the years and the message and picture are hardly decipherable. These should be avoided when buying.

Prices will vary according to the colour and/or amount of decoration. A speckled Nailsea pin will be about £40–£80; one with a combed looped decoration will be about £60–£120, and one showing a sailing ship accompanied by a lengthy verse will be about £100 or more.

Three Nailsea style rolling pins c.1860. Average length 14in
TOP: Amethyst glass, cold enamelled with the message 'Love and Be True' and a ship and anchor; £70–£80.
CENTRE: Blue rolling pin showing the flags from the Crimean War and bearing the message 'The Girl I Love'; £60–£70.
BOTTOM: Blue pin marked 'Forget Me Not' and showing the Sunderland Bridge; £70–£90.

· ROYAL ·
· BRIERLEY ·
· CRYSTAL ·
See Stevens & Williams

S

· SALTS ·

Glass salt containers have been made since the 18th century, but it was in the mid-19th century that they were made in quantity and in a great variety of shapes and sizes.

Early 19th-century salts usually consisted of small rounded bowls set on pedestal feet and were often heavily cut with vertical ribs and bands of diamond cutting (see CUTTING, GLASS). The base could be round or square, and a square 'lemon squeezer' base could be stepped or terraced. Canoe shapes, made in imitation of silver or pewter salts, were decorated with vertical fluting.

With the abolition of the Glass Tax of 1845, and the advent of pressed glass (see PRESS-MOULDED GLASS), salts were produced in their thousands. The pressed glass imitated the earlier, more expensive cut glass, and shapes were round, oval, square or boat-like. The salts stood on flat bases, had tiny knobbed feet, or copied the elaborate pedestal bases of their dearer counterparts. Bases were often additionally ornamented with star cutting.

At first the salts were made in clear glass, but they were later produced in coloured glass of blue, green, amber, red and yellow. They also appeared made in vitro-porcelain (q.v.), an opaque white or coloured glass that was intended to

LEFT: One of a pair of blue boat-shaped salts with diamond cut body and vandyke rim c.1780. Height 1¾in; £360–£400 the pair.
RIGHT: Bonnet glass salt with cut body and 'lemon squeezer' base, c.1810. Height 3in; £45–£55.

S

resemble porcelain. This was available
in various colours such as amethyst,
green, blue or black (jet), either plain or
marbled with opaque white.

Novelty salts were easily made by
pressing, and examples, such as
miniature troughs, wheelbarrows, coal
scuttles, coal trucks and even short,
solid-stemmed tobacco pipes were made
by various manufacturers. Fish such as
the dolphin were sometimes used to
decorate the pedestal bases.

Clear glass salts are easily and cheaply
found at flea markets and smaller
auctions. Check that there are no chips
to the rim or base, and that there are no
cracks concealed by the pressed pattern.

A small plain salt will cost no more
than £2 or £3; those of larger size with a
good pressed pattern in clear glass will
cost £10 upwards. Coloured opaque
glass examples will be from about £20;
while novelty salts can cost as much as
£30 or more depending on the style and
colour. Salts from about 1825, well cut
and set on square bases, will be about
£20–£60 each.

· SANDWICH ·
· GLASS ·
See American Lacy Glass

S

· SATIN · GLASS ·

To English glassmakers satin glass is a type of finish, to American glass collectors it means mother-of-pearl. It is thought that Benjamin Richardson (q.v.) first produced satin glass when he manufactured his 'Pearl Satin Ware' in about 1880. The technique, however, was perfected by Thomas Webb (q.v.) of Stourbridge and he is generally credited with the invention. In America it was made by the Mount Washington Company and the Phoenix Glass Company.

Satin glass was made by coating a finished item of cased glass (see CAMEO GLASS) with a transparent crystal glaze while it was still hot. After annealing (controlled cooling), the piece was subjected to a tank of acid vapour which 'etched' the surface to a matt satin finish.

Satin glass was made in various colours, usually cased on white, and Thomas Webb even introduced 'Rainbow Satin' which had various colours arranged in a striped pattern. The glass was mainly used for vases and posy holders, although rather light 'paperweights' can be found which resemble the sea urchin in shape. Satin glass could be left plain or decorated with a criss-cross pattern.

A satin glass vase will be expensive and, depending on size, could cost well over £100. A 'paperweight' in pink glass with a criss-cross pattern will be £60–£80.

· SCENT · · BOTTLES ·

Perfume has been known and used for over three thousand years. It was mainly employed in religious ceremonies, and frankincense and myrrh were offered as

Perfume flask with ruby decoration c.1850; £100–£200.

S

gifts at the birth of Christ. Early perfume consisted of unguents, oils and essences, and it was not until the 17th century that the Arabs distilled liquid scent, although earlier the Greeks had produced a kind of liquid perfume that was made by suspending crushed and powdered fragrances in oil.

Scent bottles, too, are pre-Christian in origin, and have been unearthed in archaeological excavations. Bottles, jars and ointment pots were made in a variety of materials: terracotta, alabaster and amber, porcelain and enamel, gold and silver. It is thought that the Egyptians were the first to make them in glass, but the mid-18th century is generally recognised as being the time when the glass scent bottle came into its own.

The English glasshouses made bottles of unsurpassed beauty in clear, blue, green and opaque white. These were lavishly enamelled and/or gilded in delicate and elaborate patterns, or enclosed in gold openwork 'cages'. By

LEFT: Red oval scent bottle with silver gilt mounts and integral vinaigrette by Samson Mordan 1878. Length 3¼in, £450–£500.
RIGHT: Octagonal scent with silver gilt mounts c.1880. Height 3in; £300–£500.

S

the early years of the 19th century the
variety of scent bottles available was
overwhelming.

Among the early bottles were the
long, narrow phials of square shape that
were filled with rosewater. These were
called (for some unknown reason)
'Oxford Lavenders'. They were usually
made in clear flint glass, but specimens
have been found in both pale and dark
blue. They were the first of the 'throw
away' bottles, not intended to be kept,
and so are often crudely decorated.
They are rarely found complete with
their stoppers.

Bristol glassmakers (see BRISTOL
GLASS) made bottles in dark blue,
emerald and, more rarely, amethyst
glass. Small Nailsea bottles (see NAILSEA
GLASS and NAILSEA-STYLE GLASS)
resembled the larger flasks and were
made with spiral or latticinio patterns in
opaque white or coloured glass.

Bottles were also made in clear glass
and these were heavily cut and/or
faceted. Cased glass (see CAMEO GLASS)
was used and cut away in a honeycomb
pattern, or carved in cameo design.

Shapes varied enormously, and
ranged between being globular, angular

LEFT: Art Deco scent
bottle in deep turquoise
blue with matching
stopper c.1930; £20–£40.
CENTRE: Perfume flask in
clear glass with ringed
neck and mushroom
stopper c.1850; £100–
£150.
RIGHT: Press-moulded
scent bottle in dark blue
glass with inner stopper of
frosted glass (cap
missing); £40–£60
complete.

S

and oval, although the teardrop shape used in ancient times continued to be popular.

The most well-known phial of the Victorian era was the faceted, double-ended scent bottle that was made between about 1850 and 1900. This was used to hold both perfume and smelling salts, the bottle being divided into two sections internally. Smelling salts had a corrosive action on the glass making it appear cloudy, so coloured glass was used. Red and dark blue were favourite colours, but green and a yellowish brown can also be found. Two colours were occasionally combined in the same bottle.

Bottles came with screw-topped caps, or there were some that relied on a tight push-on fit. The bottles sometimes had an inner glass stopper of clear glass which had been ground to fit the opening exactly, thus avoiding any spillage or leaking of the contents. Some caps were hinged on to a patent spring device that sealed the bottle securely. The caps were made in silver or gilded brass, rarely in gold. They were often ornately embossed, or could be set with precious or semi-precious stones, or with coloured glass that was cut and faceted in imitation of these.

Larger bottles were made for use on the dressing table. These could resemble miniature decanters and were fitted with cut glass stoppers that had been ground to fit. Late Victorian and Edwardian bottles were globular in shape and heavily cut in hobnail, diamond or strawberry patterns (see CUTTING, GLASS). These were occasionally mounted with silver 'shoulders' and would have large, plain or embossed caps in hallmarked silver. Cheaper alternatives were made in pressed glass (see PRESS-MOULDED

LEFT: Red onion-shaped vinaigrette in red cut glass with embossed silver mounts, used to hold small sponges soaked with perfume, c.1880. Height 1¼in; £200–£250.
CENTRE: Oval scent with floral gilt decoration and copper gilt mounts c.1780. Length 4½in; £450–£550.
RIGHT: Green tapered rectangular perfume bottle with gilt scroll decoration c.1880. Length 4in; £120–£150.

Two overlay scent bottles with embossed silver mounts c.1860.
LEFT: £360–£400;
RIGHT: £320–£360.

GLASS) and had silver-plated caps.

Early 'spray-on' perfume bottles relied on a pump action where the upstanding metal 'siphon' was sharply depressed to release a fine spray. Later, a rubber bulb and tube system was used. The bulb was encased in a silken crocheted or woven cover and was invariably tasselled. The bulb type of fitment is most often found in bottles from the 1920s and 1930s.

Art Deco styles influenced the design of scent bottles. They became angular and geometric in shape and the stopper was often the focal point. The latter could be a round disc of glass standing upright and fans, triangles and pointed spear shapes became common. Sometimes the stopper eclipsed the bottle. Sweeping 'wings' of glass curved down as if enclosing the bottle.

Frosted glass of pastel colours was frequently used, and this could be further etched in geometric or natural patterns of birds, such as the peacock. Clear glass was incised and enamelled in vivid colour combinations of green and silver or red and black. Patterns were angular and sharp; squares, triangles and stepped motifs are all distinctive of the period.

S

When buying scent bottles it is important to examine them carefully. Cut or pressed glass examples should be checked for chips and cracks. The neck and stopper should be examined for interior chips, and the stopper should be checked to make sure that it fits snugly into the neck without rocking. Make sure that any hinges are still strong as these can weaken with age and use. If a clear glass bottle is clouded, it is best left alone as it may have been used for smelling salts and nothing will remove the marks.

If buying a spray-type bottle, check that the bulb has not perished and that the woven covering is not damaged. The bulbs can be replaced, but are often difficult to track down.

Prices will vary enormously. A plain bottle in clear glass with a simple silver top will cost about £12–£15. A cut glass dressing-table flask of the Edwardian period will be about £70–£90; one in pressed glass with a plated top will cost between £15 and £25, depending on the pattern. A double-ended Victorian bottle will be £100–£200, and a small Nailsea-type flask will be about £50–£80. Art Deco bottles can be bought for as little as £20 for one in pink frosted glass, but more if the stopper is ornate. A good example of an angular shape with a geometric pattern is likely to cost between £75 and £100.

LEFT TO RIGHT: Blue double-ended scent bottle with vinaigrette end and gilt metal mounts c.1870. Length 3¾in; £250–£350.
Red double-ended perfume bottle with vinaigrette base and turquoise-studded horseshoe design on the gilt cap c.1880. Length 4in; £250–£300.
Blue opera glass scent bottle with centre hinge and gilt mounts c.1870. Length 5½in; £140–£175.
Red double-ended scent bottle with embossed gilt metal mounts c.1880. Length 5½in; £120–£150.

S

· SHIPS · IN ·
· BOTTLES ·

These nautical curiosities date from the beginning of the 19th century. It is thought that they were made by sailors during the long hours when a ship was becalmed or on lengthy sea voyages. They were often given to wives or sweethearts as mementoes or souvenirs or were sold when in port to augment the seaman's wages.

Schooners and barquentines are the sailing ships most often modelled, and these can be found with two, three, four or even five masts. The hull of the ship is usually carved from wood, and the bows will face the neck of the bottle. The masts and stays are also made of wood, with the rigging made of fine twine. Sails were uncommon on ships in bottles in the 19th century, as finding thin paper on board ship was a problem for sailors. When it was finished the vessel would be set on a sea of painted putty which gradually superseded the paper and cloth used in earlier years.

It is often the style of the ship, the accuracy of the rigging and the proportions of the masts and stays etc. that help in dating a ship in a bottle. For example, the four-masted ship first made its appearance in about 1875; five-masted ships were not constructed until after the turn of the century.

The bottles containing the ships are generally of a pale greenish blue (aqua) colour and were originally moulded wine or spirit bottles of cylindrical or oval form. The three-part mould was in use from about 1820 until about 1900, and the three seams can sometimes be detected. However, two-seamed bottles were also being made during this period, especially on the Continent. Pontil marks and a high kick up on the bottle can also indicate age. It is advisable to be wary of putting too much faith into dating the model from the age of the bottle as modern model ships can be inserted into old bottles. Any sign of plastic on the model is a giveaway and the model should be shunned.

Prices vary according to the age and quality of the model. Those with detailed deck fittings and well-proportioned masts will command a higher price. A small 20th-century ship in a rather squat bottle can be found from about £20 upwards; those of greater age over £200.

· SHOES · & · · BOOTS ·

Shoes have always been associated with good luck, especially with newly-weds, and the superstition is still in force today with old shoes being tied to the bumper of the bride and groom's car as they set off on their honeymoon. Early in the 19th century miniature examples were often given as love tokens between

Selection of late 18th and 19th century stirrup cups in the shape of boots. £50–£80 each.

courting couples. Shoes had a slightly
erotic connotation during the Victorian
era, when female feet and ankles were
hidden by long skirts. This concealment
aroused the male curiosity and snuff
boxes, pen-knives and other masculine
accessories were often made as
representations of the 'forbidden' shoe,
and pipe tampers were manufactured in
the shape of a female leg.

Miniature boots and shoes have been
made in a variety of materials such as
wood, metal, pottery and porcelain, as
well as in glass. They could be made
purely for decorative purposes or put to
a more practical use as toothpick or
match holders, match strikers or spirit
measures. They were also used as
thimble holders, pincushions, salts and
inkwells. High-heeled shoes with a
'stepped' insole were made to hold salt,
pepper and mustard pots. Larger shoes
of about eight inches (20 cm) in length
were made as flower or posy holders.
Spill vases often showed shoes set on a
square base.

There is a great variety of shoes and
boots made in pressed glass (see PRESS-
MOULDED GLASS). They include the
'Puss in Boots' type of boot, which were
made in clear glass with a frosted 'cuff'
to the boot. Cinderella-type slippers
were made in clear glass of various
colours, such as amber, dark green, dark
blue, red, pink (see CRANBERRY GLASS),
black and opaque white. They were also
made in opalescent glass (see VASELINE
GLASS) and marbled glass of green or
amethyst and white (see VITRO-
PORCELAIN GLASS). Dutch clogs, ladies'
high boots and ankle boots were also
made in glass, and lace-up shoes often
featured a small cat tucked into the
opening.

Some shoes and boots are marked
with the maker's mark (see MAKERS'

TRADEMARKS), usually Sowerby's (q.v.) and this adds interest and value.

Reproduction shoes are now being made especially in opaque white glass. These are poorly made in comparison with the Victorian examples and some can be found stamped 'Taiwan'.

Prices vary according to the style of the boot or shoe and the colour or type of glass used. Clear glass boots will be about £25 upwards; pressed glass examples with an interesting texture or colour will start at about £30–£40, more if stamped with the maker's mark. Vaseline and Cranberry glass are about £40–£50 upwards.

· SLAG · GLASS ·

This is a term which causes much confusion among collectors and even experts have divided opinions on the definition of slag glass.

The most widely held opinion is that slag glass was made by taking the scum skimmed off the surface of the molten iron used in smelting, and adding it to the glass mix. This then gave a marbled or mottled effect to the opaque glass (see VITRO-PORCELAIN GLASS) first pioneered by Sowerby's (q.v.).

However, it has also been stated that slag glass was a type of semi-opaque bottle glass produced by Sowerby's which appeared to be black in colour, although when held up to the light was actually a very dark green or purple.

· SOWERBY'S · · ELLISON · · GLASS WORKS ·

George Sowerby established the first Sowerby glassworks in Gateshead in about 1765 and by the mid-19th century the company boasted, with

S

Base of the above showing the Sowerby 'peacock' trademark and registered diamond lozenge for 18th September 1879.

some justification, that they were 'the largest manufacturers of flint glass in the kingdom'. The Ellison Street works covered a site of some five and a half acres, and the company employed up to 1000 workmen. Sowerby's operated under various names over the years, and the final title of Sowerby's Ellison Glass Works was registered in 1872.

George's son, John, had a great deal of influence on the manufacture of pressed glass (see PRESS-MOULDED GLASS) and the company had its own iron foundry which produced the moulds needed for the vast range of novelty items they manufactured. John Sowerby was, in turn, succeeded by his son John George, who was also an innovator, and John George managed the works from the early 1870s onwards.

The company's pressed glass ware was amongst the finest in the country, and in 1877 they introduced a new opaque glass which was marketed under the name of 'Vitro-Porcelain' (q.v.). This was followed by Malachite, New Marble Glass and Tortoiseshell, plus new colours of Jet, Gold Nugget and Blanc-de-Lait, an opalescent glass.

In 1881 Sowerby's patented an inner plunger for use in the making of pressed glass. This enabled the pattern to be produced on the inner surface of the article, giving an added brilliance to the clear glass.

S

The Sowerby trademark (see MAKERS' TRADEMARKS) was registered in 1876 and consists of a peacock's head with crest, although it can sometimes be mistaken for a performing seal with a ball balanced on its nose. It was applied to either the inner or outer surface of the glass and was often accompanied by a registered design lozenge (see REGISTERED DESIGN NUMBERS).

· STAINED · · GLASS ·

Although the use of stained glass in windows goes back to medieval times, it was mainly restricted to religious buildings. It became fashionable in the private home towards the end of the 19th century and continued in popularity well into the 1920s and 1930s. Stained glass in jewel colours was generally used for smaller windows such as fanlights, bathroom and lavatory windows, hall panels and roundels for the front door.

The design was traced out on to coloured glass which was then cut. The cut pieces of glass were held together with lead glazing bars. The coloured glass could be additionally enhanced by painting with enamels.

The Victorians favoured land and seascapes, while the later Art Nouveau (q.v.) period saw romantic images and figures being portrayed in misty colours. Paintings of dogs or birds shown in their natural habitat would sometimes be featured as the centrepiece of a stained glass window. The tulip motif was also popular at this time, and was often set in the corners of leaded windows or in the panels of fanlights.

In the 1920s and 1930s sunbursts and geometric designs were used for interior doors and larger windows. This period

Stained glass window showing sacred ibis and swallows among bullrushes c.1880–90, originally in a shop in the King's Road, Brighton. Height 8ft (Brighton Museum).

An interior stained glass window shown in situ, the coloured glass panels set in an arch c.1890–1910.

also favoured panels which featured billowing galleons being tossed on lively waves, or red-sailed yachts scudding before the wind. Landscapes often portrayed idyllic rural scenes.

When buying stained glass panels it is important to check that the glass is not cracked. Smaller sections can be replaced but specialists are hard to find. Any damaged pieces should, ideally, be replaced with old glass and this can be a problem. Check also that the lead bars are not weak; this can cause a 'caving in' effect which spoils the look of the panel.

Auctions are good sources for buying, but often the panels are still in their original wooden window frames and, again, expert help might be needed to free the glass.

The price depends on the age and design of the glass. A small fanlight window with coloured squares and two or three tulip motifs dating from about 1910 will cost about £20–£30 in auction. A larger piece of similar age with perhaps a central roundel or painted scenic decoration will cost £150 or more.

· STEVENS · & · · WILLIAMS ·

This glasshouse at Brierley Hill was established in the 1830s, but it was in the 1880s that it achieved recognition with the manufacture of cameo glass (q.v.) which rivalled that of Webb's (q.v.). In 1880 John Northwood (q.v.) was employed as art director and the company flourished.

In 1886 the company produced a new glass called Jewel which was threaded glass work made in brilliant colours of ruby and gold. The depth of colour achieved by the factory was further enhanced with the introduction of Dragon's Blood, a rich, strong red, in

1891.

At the turn of the century the company produced Silveria, a method whereby small pieces of silver foil or silver mica were enclosed between two layers of glass. This gave an attractive flecked appearance to the coloured glass. This was later followed by Alexandrite, a type of cased glass.

In the early 1900s and again in 1921, Stevens & Williams produced a gold iridescent glass very similar to the iridised Carnival glass (q.v.) that was being produced in America. John Northwood's son Harry emigrated to the United States in 1880 and his company became one of the largest manufacturers of Carnival glass. It was a coincidence perhaps that his father was the art director for Stevens & Williams.

In 1932 Keith Murray, a noted designer, was retained by the company, now known as Royal Brierley Crystal. Murray was influenced in his designs by the modern glass being produced in Scandinavia at this time and the cutting and quality of glass made before 1850. This gave his work a stylish simplicity of form which, combined with little or no decoration, produced a range of glassware that was both innovative yet comfortable to live with.

There are several marks (see MAKERS' TRADEMARKS) for Stevens & Williams and Brierley Crystal. Keith Murray glass was considered a separate entity and each piece was stamped or etched with Murray's facsimile signature.

Fruit bowl with cut diamond pattern c.1920. Marked on base with the Brierley Crystal fleur-de-lys trademark; £40–£60.

t

· TANTALUS ·
See Decanters

· TAZZAS ·

These glass cake plates, also known as comports, were made in large quantities from about 1750, and many fine examples can be found made in pressed glass (see PRESS-MOULDED GLASS).

The tazza usually consists of a large flat plate, although it can sometimes be slightly dished, set on a footed stem. The stem could be from one to five inches (2–12 cm) in length, so that the tazzas are of varying heights. The rim of the plate usually stood slightly proud and could be lightly frilled. The more dished tazzas sometimes had a deep, wavy edge.

Those in clear glass are usually very heavily patterned in imitation of cut glass, or could perhaps have a moulded design of lozenges or elongated hearts. Frosted examples might have a pattern of clear glass circles and radiating rays or could be decorated with an interesting Greek key design, such as those made by Molineaux Webb.

Coloured glass tazzas can be found in yellow and turquoise Pearline (q.v.), sometimes with an added hint of opalescence (see VASELINE GLASS). Dark green, ruby red and amber tazzas often had a basket weave pattern.

Top view of a tazza set on three short feet, made in moulded glass c.1920. Diameter 9in; £10–£15.

Two glass tazzas with flat platforms and hollow Silesian stems, with domed and folded feet c.1750. Diameter 9¾in and 7¾in; £280–£350 and £250–£320.

Many tazzas carry a registered mark (see REGISTERED DESIGN NUMBERS) which is a guide to identifying and dating. This can often be missed by the naked eye so it is always best to run the fingers along the surface of the glass as the raised letters and numbers can be felt more easily than they are seen.

When buying, check for rim chips. If the rim of the tazza is 'toothed', any damage can easily be missed. The foot is also a vulnerable area.

Prices can vary enormously. Boot sales and flea markets are ideal hunting grounds for clear glass examples, and prices here will start at only a few pounds. Heavily patterned tazzas will cost about £15 upwards at an antiques fair, and if made of coloured glass, will be about £30–£40. Opalescent and Pearline examples will cost perhaps twice as much; 18th-century tazzas will be £200–£250 upwards.

· TIFFANY ·
LOUIS COMFORT
(1848–1933)

Probably the most famous glassmaker in America, Tiffany was the son of a fashionable New York jeweller, Charles Lewis Tiffany.

During his visits to Paris in the 1880s, Tiffany had been very impressed by the Art Nouveau movement. He greatly admired the work produced by Gallé (q.v.), the French craftsman, and in 1885 he formed a new company, the Tiffany Glass Company. In 1892 the name was changed to the Tiffany Glass and Decorating Company, and in 1890 he set up the Tiffany Studios in New York.

Tiffany's first work was with stained glass, mosaics and tiles and these ranged from examples made in clear, jewel-like

Sweetmeat stand in Vaseline and opaque white glass, the rim engraved with a fruiting vine. Etched underneath with 'LCT Favrile' and the number NM50. Height 7¾in; £2000+.

colours to those that glowed with a subdued opalescence or had a metallic iridised surface. The leaded glass windows were never painted, but relied on the random colours that swirled romantically, being shaded by the varying thickness of the glass.

The stylish lamps are perhaps Tiffany's most famous 'trademark', and these are amongst the most collectable of his work, although the making of leaded glass shades was already in existence when he began production. Tiffany's shades were made in a mosaic of rich colours and were combined with bronze bases. They followed the naturalistic theme so popular with the Art Nouveau designers of the day, and depicted insects such as the dragonfly, spiders' webs and flowers such as the water lily, lotus, apple blossom and wistaria. Desk lamps, table lamps, standard lamps, chandeliers and ceiling lights were all produced in dazzling colours and elegant shapes.

Favrile glass consisted of glass with an iridised metallic lustre finish which gave a rainbow effect to the basic colours of dark blue, green, silver or gold. The glass achieved its colour by the addition of various metallic oxides, and the lustre effect was obtained by introducing the salts of metallic oxides into the molten metal. The metallic content was brought to the surface by reduction. A chloride was then sprayed on to the surface giving it a refractive 'crackle' finish.

The molten glass was free-blown into shape (see BLOWN AND BLOW-MOULDED GLASS). This gave an individuality of form to each piece and the glass-blowers were often allowed a certain amount of licence in their work and thus produced vases of elongated flower form or of similar sinuous shape. Plain shapes were decorated with patterns of leaves or

Small moulded bowl with opaque green, amber and blue decoration. Etched on base, 'LCT Favrile'. Height 2¼ in; £300.

Pair of glass salts in Favrile glass, complete with bronze spoons and in original velvet box c.1900. Height of salts 2¼in; £1000+.

vines; perhaps the most well-known pattern is that of the peacock feather with its stylised 'eyes'. The feather effect was achieved by combing the glass, the eye was added to the parison, then smoothed out on the marver.

The interest in natural forms and designs led to the introduction of agate glass. This marbled stone effect was produced by mixing various colours of opaque glass at a low temperature. The heat was not so great that the metal mingled absolutely and the result was a variegated, layered glass. This was then cut or faceted in imitation of natural agate.

Cypriot glass was also iridescent, usually yellow in colour, and had a rough, pitted surface in imitation of glass that had been buried for many centuries. This pitted effect was obtained by rolling the blown glass over a layer of crushed glass before adding the lustre finish. Lava glass also had a rough surface, but this was achieved by dripping runs and blobs of molten glass on to the surface. The molten glass had been mixed with basalt or talc and gave a suitably 'volcanic' effect. The finished piece was then polished and lustred.

Reactive glass was made by reheating translucent glass in the furnace. It then changed colour and became iridescent.

Millefiori or paperweight glass (see PAPERWEIGHTS) was made by lightly touching the molten glass with a bundle of prepared canes in floret or organic shapes. A thin cross-section of the canes then fused itself to the body of the piece, forming the pattern. The article would then be reheated to absorb the florets and then lustred. These millefiori patterns were generally large and well spaced out, with the florets rather 'pulled' in appearance. The lustred Favrile paperweight vases are extremely sought after.

Much of Tiffany's glass has been copied by designers and manufacturers over the years. Fortunately most of the Tiffany glass was marked or signed. The early numbered pieces were marked with the prefix 'x'. Favrile glass was signed or initialled 'Tiffany' or 'LCT'. Later pieces of this glass carried a letter as a prefix or suffix, and it is possible to date Tiffany glass from these. The prefixes A to N were used from 1896–1900, and P–Z between 1901 and 1905. Suffixes A–N date from 1906–12, and P–Z give a date of 1913–20. The prefix O was for special orders only and is rarely found.

· TRADEMARKS ·
See Makers' Trademarks

· TRINKET · SETS ·
These sets were an essential part of the bedroom fittings for ladies of quality, and during the Victorian and Edwardian era they were produced in brilliant cut glass as well as in china and porcelain. The trinket pots and scent bottles would have glass lids and stoppers, or ones made in silver or EPNS (electroplated nickel silver).

The trinket set was designed for the dressing table and consisted of a varying number of items. The main tray was large and accommodated a pin tray and ring stand. Lidded trinket pots, usually two of large or small size, would be made to match, and sometimes a hair tidy was included. This had a large hole in the metal lid into which the loose combings were pushed for tidiness. A perfume bottle or flask was often part of the set, together with a pair of candlesticks.

With new techniques in moulded and pressed glass (see BLOWN AND BLOW-MOULDED GLASS and PRESS-MOULDED GLASS) trinket sets became available to all and by the 1920s and 1930s they were seen on almost every dressing table.

Sets were made in pastel colours of pink, blue, green and amber, or in the darker, more dramatic colours and Art Deco designs of Cloud glass (q.v.). This was produced by Davidson's (q.v.) in 1922 and was made in brown and amber, red (rare), purple, blue, grey (rare) and green.

Glass trinket sets were much used and were therefore prone to damage. Check when buying that ring stands still have their branches and that none of the other pieces is chipped. The inner surfaces of lids and rims of containers were particularly vulnerable. If the pots and bottles have silver caps, check for the hallmark; if plated, ensure that the

Art Deco trinket set in deep amber glass c.1930; £30–£60.

metal is not scratched, yellowed or worn.

A complete set of large tray, pin tray, ring stand, two trinket pots, and a pair of candlesticks, made in clear moulded glass of the 1920s or 1930s can be found surprisingly cheaply for about £20–£30. One in coloured glass in Art Deco style will be about £40–£60. An elaborate Edwardian set in cut crystal will be about £100, more if the lids are of silver.

· TUMBLERS ·

These straight-sided drinking glasses can vary in size from small tumblers only one-eighth of a pint to the standard glass which usually holds between nine and eleven fluid ounces, or about half a pint.

Late Victorian pressed glass tumblers (see PRESS-MOULDED GLASS) are generally thick and heavy as production techniques were not sophisticated enough to manufacture glasses of the required thinness without causing damage to the rims. Patterns on these early glasses are not as sharp as on flat items due to the technical difficulties, but nevertheless are superior to the cheap moulded (see BLOWN AND BLOW-MOULDED GLASS) tumblers that were later produced in their thousands.

By the turn of the century, thinner glasses were being produced and these were finely etched with elegant designs

LEFT: Tumbler with concentric moulded rings c.1780; £250–£275.
CENTRE: Tumbler engraved 'George and Mary Owen 1835' and with a floral band; £70–£90.
RIGHT: Tumbler with hatched engraved band and the monogram R.A.R.; £80–£90.

Group of four tumblers from the 1930s, etched in various patterns of scrolls, diamonds and foliage. £2–£10 each, more if in sets of six.

rather than relying on a pressed pattern for appeal. Stars were very popular, as was the Greek key design. Other patterns include an etched diamond design bordered with scrolling and a wide border of overlapping circles.

This style of glass was copied in the 1930s and was widely sold in branches of Woolworths. These glasses can often be confused with those of the earlier period. Less often seen are the Edwardian glasses prettily decorated with a pattern or flowers and foliage, etched in fine detail. Edwardian glasses could also be slightly waisted, making them even more attractive.

With some searching a matching set of tumblers can be collected for very little cost, and with patience a whole suite of glasses can be built up. When buying check for rim chips. The rims are sometimes ground down so a very straight edge to the rim should be regarded with suspicion. However, if the glass is otherwise perfect this restoration may well be acceptable.

Prices can range from about £1 for a heavy moulded Victorian tumbler to about £5-£10 for one in well-wrought pressed glass. Edwardian tumblers will each be about £5 or £8 upwards, 1930s copies about £3–£5 each. (See also DRINKING GLASSES.)

· VASELINE ·
· GLASS ·

This glass exactly resembles its name. If a jar of ordinary Vaseline jelly or ointment is held up to the light it will show a central oily yellow opalescence and this is what Vaseline glass looks like. Some people prefer to call it opalescent glass, but that can refer to the opalescent glass made in various colours whereas the name Vaseline glass is applied only to the pale creamy-yellow variety.

Vaseline glass vase with shaded green rim and clear trails of pinched glass. Height 5½in; £30–£50.

The colour was achieved by the addition of uranium to the mix before reheating the metal. Depending on how much the glass was reheated, the colour would vary from a pale cream to a deeper yellow, although Bohemian glass (q.v.) reflected a slightly richer yellow which could almost be an acid green. Vaseline glass could also be prettily shaded, going from an almost clear base through to a deeper coloured rim, or it could be of an overall primrose colour with little or no shading, the opalescence seen only when the piece is held to the light.

Although Vaseline glass was thought to be inferior to other shades of decorative glass, it was very much favoured by the Victorians. It was used mainly for smaller items, and most pieces found today consist of table ornaments such as large and small épergnes (q.v.), candlesticks, spill vases, posy holders and small flower vases, and tableware such as cream and sugar sets, butter dishes, sweetmeat and bon-bon dishes.

Apart from the épergnes, most of these items were made in pressed glass (see PRESS-MOULDED GLASS) and will often bear the mark of the maker (see MAKERS' TRADEMARKS).

The Victorians and Edwardians used to 'dress' their dining tables both during and between meals. One striking centrepiece that is shown in a copy of the 1907 catalogue of the Army and Navy Stores is called 'The New "Maypole" Table Decoration', although similar items had been made by both Webb's (q.v.) in about 1900, and Richardson's (q.v.) who called their version 'Rusticana'.

The centrepiece consisted of several small cylindrical vases resembling the trunk of a tree which were complete with small knobbly projections or twig-like nodules. The feet of the vases consisted of small twisted 'roots' that splayed out to support the 'trunk'. These vases were made in several sizes from about six inches (15 cm) in height to a large fourteen inches (35 cm). Each vase was linked to the larger central vase, maypole style, by a narrow ribbon, the loops being attached to the small projections. The catalogue advises that the 'Rustic Glass Vase complete with

Two 'Rustic' table ornaments with twig-like nodules on the trunk and root-like feet. Height 4½in; £12–£18.

Small lily or tulip vase on clear glass foot. Height 7in; £30–£40.

red and white silk ribbon' was available for eighteen shillings and sixpence (92½p). The central vase could also be dual- or multi-branched, and was occasionally made in Cranberry glass (q.v.) without any opalescence.

Vaseline glass was also used in jewellery, mostly for beads (q.v.) and necklaces. The beads can be round or faceted, combined with spandrels of crystal, or tiny beads of black glass.

The discrepancy over the definition of Vaseline glass can confuse beginners who may be misled by the yellow Pearline (q.v.) glass which has an opalescence similar to Vaseline glass but which is more acid yellow in colour, more opaque and of heavier weight. Oily green glass is also sometimes mistakenly called Vaseline, and although this does have a certain richness of colour and a hint of yellow to it, it lacks the opalescence of true Vaseline glass.

When buying Vaseline glass, especially the rustic variety, it is important to look for damage. The protrusions on the 'trunk' are easily snapped off, and the 'feet' or 'roots' are frequently missing or badly chipped. Cracks show up fairly easily when held up to the light.

Prices vary accordingly to the item. A cream and sugar set of small size will cost between £40 and £60; a single rustic ornament will be about £18–£25 depending on size, but a many-branched example will be about £40–£60, again depending on size.

Vaseline glass beads can be bought at auction for about £10–£15; around £15–£25 at an antiques fair. Check that the beads are matching in colour and not chipped or cracked, and that the silk thread is not frayed. The separating knots should not be worn, as re-stringing can prove expensive.

Fluted vase with shaded opalescence and root-like feet. Late Victorian. Height 3¾in; £30–£50.

· VITRO- · · PORCELAIN · · GLASS ·

This was a new type of glass produced in 1877 by Sowerby's (q.v.) using cryolite spar as a major ingredient. It was a dense, opaque glass that closely resembled china or glazed earthenware. It was first made in white (opal), turquoise and cream (Queen's Ivory Ware) and in 1880 other colours were added to the range, such as yellow (Giallo), 'Aesthetic' green, Gold and Blue Nugget, red and, later, Jet, a dense black. The pressed patterns in this new glass showed up particularly well.

An interesting variation was Malachite. This resembled the natural stone and was made in colours of brown and blue, as well as the more authentic green. In 1882 Sowerby's introduced tortoiseshell, followed by New Marble Glass which was also available in amethyst.

The new glass was copied by other manufacturers but Sowerby examples can usually be identified by the maker's mark pressed into the piece (see MAKERS' TRADEMARKS).

All manner of items were made, such as fruit bowls, sweetmeat dishes and baskets, posy holders, flower troughs and vases, candlesticks, spill holders and so on.

Prices vary according to the size, colour and pattern of the piece. Aesthetic green and yellow, for example, are rare colours, and a modest spill vase in yellow or green will be about £50–£60. A small malachite posy holder of square design will cost about £35–£45; a tiny basket about two and a half inches (6 cm) high made in marbled glass will be about £30–£40.

Pair of spill vases by Sowerby in rare aesthetic green c.1879. Height 4in; £150–£200.

Sowerby trademark and date diamond for 14 August 1879 marked on the base of the spill vases shown above.

· WALKING ·
· STICKS ·

Two Nailsea style walking sticks with red, white and blue colour twists c.1860. Length 39in; *LEFT*: £160–£200; *RIGHT*: £140–£160.

These glass novelties were made by the workmen in the glass houses in their spare time and as a demonstration of their skill (see FRIGGERS). They were not intended for practical use but would be shown at exhibitions or on parades. In the house they would be hung on the wall for decoration, and those of a superstitious leaning would take them down each morning and carefully wipe and polish them. The theory was that glass rods attracted germs so when the stick was cleaned the germs were disposed of and the family protected.

There is surprising variety in walking sticks. They can be plain or of a barley sugar twist shape, and have hooked or knobbed handles. The plain examples could have several bands of colour, bright barber pole stripes, or twisted threads of red, white and blue glass in Nailsea style (see NAILSEA GLASS and NAILSEA-STYLE GLASS). Hollow sticks were sometimes filled with sweets such as the tiny granular 'hundreds and thousands'.

Glass walking sticks are very prone to damage and the tip of both base and handle should be carefully examined when buying. Barley sugar twist sticks should be checked for any chipping which can be easily overlooked.

Prices will vary according to design. A walking stick of barley sugar stick twist design in pale green glass can be found at auction for about £50–£100. Those with barber pole stripes or attractively knobbed ends will cost over £150.

Pale green walking stick with latticinio threads in white glass c.1880. Length 39in; £100–£150.

· WEBB ·
THOMAS & SONS

The first Webb glassworks was set up at Amblecote in 1837. Thomas Webb had previously been in partnership with two of the Richardson brothers as Richardson & Webb (see RICHARDSONS, THE) but the company was dissolved in 1836. In 1856 Webb moved to Dennis Park where he produced both crystal and coloured glass. Thomas Webb died in 1869 and the company was run by his two sons, Wilkes and Charles.

Webb's are perhaps most associated with cameo glass (q.v.) and the factory produced some excellent pieces, employing George and Thomas Woodall, the finest artists in cameo work at that time. In 1876 Wilkes Webb commissioned John Northwood (q.v.) to make the Dennis Vase in cameo glass. Known also as the Pegasus Vase, it stood 21 inches (53 cm) high and showed scenes of Venus and her attendants, with the head and shoulders of the winged horse as the handles and the complete body as the lid.

Webb's experimented with the use of acid etching in cameo glass as well as employing the traditional engraving tools. So successful were their techniques that they produced cameo glass which was made of three layers, an improvement on the two layers previously carved.

In 1886 Webb's acquired the rights to produce Burmese glass (q.v.) in England. The glass mix recipe was altered slightly, producing a glass of a richer hue than the American glass, and the finished product was called Queen's Burmese. The creamy yellow glass with its pink shading was often signed (see MAKERS' TRADEMARKS).

Base of a fairylight with crimped edge and painted floral band c.1890. Marked inside 'Clarkes', and made by Webb. Height 2¾in.

· WINDOW ·
· GLASS ·

Nailsea crown glass
garden cloche c.1810.
Height 8½in; £70–£90.

In the early 19th century there were
two methods of making window glass.
Sheet glass was made by blowing the
molten metal into a long cylinder in a
flattening kiln. The glass was then
reheated and opened out into a large flat
sheet before being finally cooled. It was
not until the early 20th century that
glass sheets were made by continuous
rolling.

Crown glass was made by gathering a
large lump of molten glass on to the
blowing iron and blowing it into a
sphere. After reheating, the sphere was
then rotated rapidly on a pontil rod until
it formed a large, flat but slightly
concave disc. This table, as it was
known, could be as much as four feet
(1.2 m) in diameter. After it had cooled,
the glass was cut into squares or panes.
The central 'bull' or 'bullion', where the
pontil rod had been attached, was
regarded as waste and was sold off
cheaply as a 'second'. It was usually
then fitted into the windows of poorer
dwellings as a 'bull's eye' window. The
waste from the circumference of the
table was used as cullet.

Window glass was usually of a pale
green colour and apart from being used
for windows, it was also used to make
domestic wares such as bottles (q.v.),
jugs and bowls, rolling pins (q.v.) and
glass cloches. It was also used for
novelties and ornamental pieces such as

Nailsea crown window
glass cucumber
straightener c.1850.
Length 18in; £90–£120.

miniature hats (see FRIGGERS), walking sticks (q.v.), flasks, pipes (q.v.) and even door stops (see PAPERWEIGHTS).

· WINE ·
· GLASSES ·
See Drinking Glasses

· WITCH · BALLS ·

These spherical hollow glass balls were made from the 18th century onwards. They were purely ornamental and it is thought that they were made as novelties or friggers (q.v.) by the workmen. It is not clear how they got their name, but they were hung up over windows or doorways by the superstitious to ward off the evil eye and to bring good luck.

The balls had either an opening which could be corked or an integral knob for ease of hanging. Some Nailsea-style balls (see NAILSEA GLASS and NAILSEA-STYLE GLASS) had a matching glass vase which supported the ball. They were made in coloured glass of dark blue, green or cranberry (q.v.) or could be clear with spiralled threads of coloured glass. Some were silvered inside.

Witch balls from the 19th century made in plain coloured glass will cost about £50–£100; those with a Nailsea-style decoration will be about the same price.

LEFT TO RIGHT: Amethyst witch ball of bottle shape c.1860. Diameter 4½in; £50–£70.
Witch ball with green silvered body and metal cap c.1860. Diameter 6in; £50–£70.
Opaque white witch ball with blue looping c.1860. Diameter 3¼in; £50–£70.
Witch ball in clear blue glass c.1860. Diameter 5¼in; £40–£50.

glossary

ACID POLISHING: A matt surface on glass achieved by dipping it into hydrofluoric and sulphuric acid.

ANNEALING: The controlled cooling of glass. If cooled too quickly it would crack and/or shatter.

AVENTURINE GLASS: Glass made in imitation of aventurine quartz by adding small flakes of gold or copper to the molten metal. Also known as Spangled glass, sometimes as Goldstone.

BATCH: The mixture of raw materials which, when heated, form glass.

BLOWING-IRON: A long thin iron tube on to which a gather of glass would be placed for blowing into shape.

CASED GLASS: Glass having two or more layers, designed for cameo cutting.

CRACKLED GLASS: An interesting 'broken ice' effect achieved by plunging the hot glass into cold water.

CRYSTAL: General term for lead potash glass.

CULLET: Broken or reject glass which was cleaned and re-used.

ENAMELLING: Glass with a low melting point was often used as decoration on other objects, such as small metal boxes. When used on glass objects, the 'liquid' glass was painted on, then refired briefly to fuse it to the body of the piece.

ENGRAVING: A method of applying a pattern to glass. The three methods include: diamond point, where the design was 'scratched' into the glass using a hand-held tool; stipple engraving, where hundreds of tiny dots were 'hammered' into the glass to form the pattern; and wheel engraving, where the object was coated with an abrasive mixture and held against a rotating disc.

ETCHING: Where the design was put on to glass by applying acid. The item would first be coated with an acid-resisting wax, the design cut into the wax, then the piece was dipped into acid. This 'ate' the pattern into the glass.

FIRE POLISHING: A rapid reheating of pressed glass items at the glory-hole or furnace mouth to smooth the surface and remove any mould lines.

FLASHED GLASS: A thin coating or staining of coloured glass applied to clear glass before cutting.

FLINT GLASS: Good quality crystal glass using lead oxide as an ingredient. Also, a general term for colourless glass.

GATHER: A blob of molten glass taken up on the pontil rod or blowing iron.

GESSO: A composition of whiting, linseed oil and size. Used thinly as a layer on mirror and picture frames prior to their being gilded, painted or lacquered. Also used as relief moulding on furniture as a substitution for ornamental carved wood.

GLORY HOLE: A small furnace set up for fire polishing.

GOLDSTONE: See Aventurine.

glossary

KICK UP: The deep indentation at the base of a bottle.

KNOP(PED): A knob of glass used decoratively, as on the stems of wine glasses.

LATTICINIO: Threads of white or coloured glass used in the glass in a lattice pattern.

LEAD GLASS: Another word for flint glass.

LEAD OXIDE: See Flint Glass.

LEHR: A long tunnel-like oven used for controlled cooling (annealing) of the glass. The very high temperature at one end would gradually give way to room temperature at the other.

LUSTRE: An iridescent finish applied to glass and achieved by spraying the glass with a mixture of metallic salts before refiring.

MARVER: A large polished metal plate on to which the gather would be rolled prior to blowing.

METAL: The trade term for molten and (less frequently) for finished glass.

MILLEFIORI: Literally, a thousand flowers.

OVERLAY: Another term for cased glass.

PARISON MOULD: A mould used in glassmaking which formed the initial or embryo shape of the piece before it was blown.

PONTIL MARK: A rough piece of glass on the base of items that have been attached to a pontil rod. Sometimes ground down to a shallow depression.

PONTIL ROD: A long iron rod used to pick up a gather of glass for pressing, or for picking up (hot) items for fire polishing. Also known as a punty iron.

PRUNT: Small blobs of glass, usually raspberry-shaped, used decoratively.

PUNTY-IRON: Another name for a pontil rod.

SODA GLASS: A cheaper glass than lead glass, using silica and sodium carbonate.

SPANGLED GLASS: Another name for Aventurine glass.

SPATTER GLASS: A glass which combines different colours in an attractive streaky manner.

SPELTER: A metal alloy composed mainly of zinc.

TRANSFER PRINTING: A method of printing on ceramics or glass whereby the pattern was etched on to copper plates before being printed on tissue and then transferred on to the item which was being decorated.

index

·ACKNOWLEDGEMENTS·

Any book on antiques is improved by the addition of photographs and this applies particularly to one written on glass. I am, therefore, greatly indebted to Peter Greenhalf A.R.P.S., who took the superb photographs that illustrate the text of this book.

Many of the items shown are from the personal collections of fellow glass lovers, with museums and dealers in the antiques trade also helping out, as well as supplying additional invaluable information. I would like to express my thanks to the following: Annette Antiques, Lincoln; Stella Beddoe of the Royal Pavilion Art Gallery and Museum, Brighton; Malcolm Davey; the Frank & Shirley Reference Collection of Carnival Glass at the John Street Antiques Centre, Luton; Victoria Williams of the Hastings Museum and Art Gallery, Hastings, Sussex; Ann Lingard of Rope Walk Antiques, Rye, Sussex; Josie Marsden at the George Street Antiques Centre, St Albans; Christopher Maxwell-Stewart, St Leonards, East Sussex; Auriol Miller; and Barry Muncey.

Last, but by no means least, I am indebted to Wing Commander R. G. Thomas, M.B.E., R.A.F. (Retd), of Somervale Antiques, 6 Radstock Road, Midsomer Norton, Bath, who supplied an enormous number of items for photography and gave me the benefit of his vast knowledge and wide experience in dealing in glass.
Muriel M. Miller.